confident
teens

confident
teens

how to raise a positive, confident
and happy teenager

Gael Lindenfield

Thorsons

Thorsons
An Imprint of HarperCollins*Publishers*
77–85 Fulham Palace Road,
Hammersmith, London W6 8JB

The Thorsons website address is:
www.thorsons.com

Thorsons is a trademark of
HarperCollins Publishers Limited.

First published by Thorsons
This edition published 2001
3 5 7 9 10 8 6 4 2

© Gael Lindenfield

Gael Lindenfield asserts the moral right
to be identified as the author of this work

Text illustrations by Harry Venning

A catalogue record for this book
is available from the British Library

ISBN 0 00 710062 0

Printed and bound in Great Britain by
Martins the Printers Limited, Berwick upon Tweed

Dedication

To my husband, Stuart, who has been the most supportive co-parent I could ever have hoped to have. His optimism, down-to-earth wisdom and sense of fun helped transform many a moment of angst into a positive, uplifting experience.

Acknowledgements

Oh where to begin and who to leave out, those are the questions!

I feel indebted to so many people for the wisdom I have gathered on this subject during the course of my life. I even feel beholden to the people who crushed my own confidence in my childhood! Without that very personal experience of the pain that accompanies a lack of confidence, I would probably have never fully appreciated the pleasures that an abundance of it can bring!

But fortunately, there have been many more positive forces at work since that time. Certainly without some of these, this book in particular could never have been written. The first voice to sow its initial seed came from Moira O'Reilly, a great friend and my PR advisor in Ireland. Thank you so much Moira for persisting with your encouragement for a further six years!

I also owe a similar debt of gratitude to Wanda Whiteley, my editor at Thorsons, who (in perhaps a slightly gentler but no less persistent vein!) sang the same song in England.

In addition, I'd like to make special mention of all of the parents and teens who took the trouble to respond to the questionnaire I sent out before writing this book. The wisdom contained in your responses deserves a book all to itself. Thank you so much for your honesty and your inspiring examples of good parenting in spite of so many setbacks and challenges.

Finally, the people whom I could never thank enough would be my daughters, Susannah and Laura. I feel that much of my learning on this subject was acquired jointly with them. There were many times when my husband and myself clearly did not know the answers (in spite of reading all the books we could find!). We all had to experiment until we found a 'formula' that worked. I know that it was this hands-on experience of working through our difficulties that helped me most to help other parents and eventually to write this book.

Contents

Introduction

Would you believe that it has taken me a full six years to summon up the confidence to write this book?!

And that is in spite of:

- having re-built my own confidence from the rockiest of rock bottoms
- achieving a successful career for the past 25 years by helping others to build theirs
- receiving streams of letters and calls from grateful readers of one of my earlier books, *Confident Children*
- being asked countless times by parents, teachers, youth workers and editors to write this book

and, most importantly:

- having launched two highly confident teenagers into the world.

So, *'what was your problem?'* you might well ask. In a nutshell, I felt overwhelmed by the responsibility of taking on such a vital task, knowing that never in a million years could it be done perfectly!

Then, thanks to a flash of insight, I realized that was exactly how so many parents of teens currently feel.

The actual task of building enough confidence in children to enable them to thrive in today's world is *just* as daunting as writing a book on the subject. The difference is that most parents have to tackle their task without the benefit of hindsight or professional expertise – and they don't have the luxury of saying 'No!'

So applying the magic of the 'Just Do It!' approach, I started to write. Once in the flow, my problem changed. I found that I had enough confidence and material to write five volumes! The big problem facing me now was how to contain myself and my subject. I knew I had to condense my thoughts into one slim book because how many parents have the time and energy to read much else? I hope that you will find this book easier to read and more practical to use than the encyclopaedia that could have emerged!

Above all, teens need confident parents to set them an inspiring example. Therefore, one of my main aims in writing this book is to provide a self-help tool to build and boost *your* confidence as a parent. So, although for obvious reasons the content of the book centres around difficulties you may encounter, please don't lose sight of the positives. The fact is that the vast majority of parents have a great time parenting their teens. I can honestly say that the years I spent with my teens were the most exciting and rewarding of my life. Of course there were some tantrums and traumas – I expected that. (Aren't the dire warnings about adolescent angst and anti-social behaviour everywhere?) But what I didn't expect was the amazing degree of fun, companionship and life-broadening experiences that totally outweighed the difficulties. I hope this proves to be your experience of parenting your teen as well.

If from time to time it doesn't, don't take all the blame upon yourself. Doing this will neither help you nor your teen. Although as parents we have a powerful role to play in building the confidence of our children, we have to accept that many other factors can be highly influential as well. It is hard enough for adults to feel good about themselves in our current world. More and more people are feeling daunted by the competitive pressure that globalization has brought and the ever-moving goalposts in the world of work. At the same time, vast numbers of us are feeling personal failures. It is proving so hard to keep on top of the hectic lifestyle we lead and live up to the images of perfection that the mass media floods our minds with. Seeing so many adults around them 'losing it', is it any wonder that teenagers often feel that they have little chance in the jungle either?

In addition, a number of you will have inherited extra obstacles. Your child may, for example, have a genetic pre-disposition which has stacked the cards against them. A shy or volatile temperament or an intellectual or physical disability can make it much harder for a child to achieve their potential and integrate into their community. Alternatively, your family may have had to struggle with social or economic disadvantages, which none of you asked for – or deserved! Teenagers from minority ethnic groups or from poor communities often have good reason to have less self-esteem and also have fewer chances to acquire the skills that help build confidence.

Finally, please also remember that no one but a saint could sail through these challenging years without frequently running into problems and breaking many of the Golden Rules, which I discuss later. Confident parents are not perfect people. They know they have faults and make mistakes. But they persevere in spite of their own imperfections and setbacks. They do not remain daunted by challenges for long – when they decide to 'go for it', they embrace the challenges and enjoy them!

part one

Raising Confident Teens:
Everything You Need to Know!

What Exactly is Confidence?

'She's an intelligent, talented girl and a pleasure to have in the class, but she could do so much more if only she had more confidence.'

'Yes, he does get picked on. If he was a bit more confident they'd probably leave him alone.'

'Why didn't she tell me this herself? If I'd known before I could have helped. The trouble is that she's so quiet. If she'd only speak up more in class.'

'There's nothing stopping him but himself. He's got to believe he can do it. He's too much of a worrier.'

These are the kind of remarks that have sent parents running to see me. Their cry of despair and guilt is almost invariably the same:

'I know she needs more confidence, but what can I do? I've tried everything. We couldn't love the children more than we do. It's not that we want them to be super-successful – we just want them to be happy and give them the best start in life. Where have we gone wrong?'

The first task, as in any kind of problem-solving process, is to stop beating ourselves up about what we have or haven't done. The second is to break down what appears to be an impossibly giant problem into manageable proportions. If you promise to take care of the first, I will now attempt to help you with the second!

Several years ago, after carefully observing the characteristics and behaviour of confident and not-so-confident people and studying the research, I decided that self-confidence is actually a package. In that package we would expect to find a *good-enough* supply of eight key ingredients. Some of these are personal qualities, which feed our inner confidence, and others are learned social skills, which enable us to handle the outside world in a confident manner. If we are lucky enough to have a *good-enough* supply of *all* eight of these ingredients, we seem to have an extra boost of personal power and *feel* and *appear* to be what I call Super Confident.

8 Key Ingredients of Super Confidence

Inner confidence:
- self-love (adopting self-nurturing behaviour and lifestyle)
- self-knowledge (reflecting on feelings, thoughts and behaviour)
- clear goals (having a strong sense of purpose)
- positive thinking (expecting and looking for good experiences and outcomes)

Outer confidence:
- communication skills (communicating effectively with people)
- self-presentation ('looking the part' of a confident person)
- assertiveness (expressing needs directly and insisting upon one's rights)
- emotional control (keeping 'the upper hand' on emotions)

Meet the Super Confident Teen

Now I'd like you to use your imagination to visualize some teenagers brimming with 'super confidence'. I am aware that, unless you inhabit a different planet to me, you might find it difficult to bring this image to mind. So here are some clues. This is what you should be imagining:

1. *Being full of SELF-LOVE, you would see them:*
- eating highly nutritious, well-balanced, regular meals; keeping away from all forms of junk food and going very easy on toxic drinks
- saying a firm 'No' to debilitating late nights and all night raves
- sharing their achievements openly and proudly with the rest of the world and never putting themselves down

2. *Having a high degree of SELF-KNOWLEDGE, you would see them:*
- looking at ease if you saw them confronted with a difficult decision or dilemma because they have such a clear idea of what they believe to be right and wrong
- achieving goals because they know exactly what their strengths and weaknesses are, and they would play on one and avoid using the other

3. *Having CLEAR GOALS, you would see them:*
- leaping out of bed with enthusiasm each morning because they would be pursuing a vivid 'life-dream'
- working purposefully. You would never catch them dithering about what to do next

4. *Being great POSITIVE THINKERS, you would see them:*
- chatting optimistically about their future plans
- looking for the best qualities in the people around them

5. Being highly SKILLED COMMUNICATORS, you would see them:
- listening carefully and patiently before saying their piece
- presenting their case in an articulate and appealing manner

6. Being skilled at SELF-PRESENTATION, you would see them:
- choosing to wear clean, eye-catching clothes
- refusing to wear or be sold clothes that didn't suit them even though they might be the latest 'in' look
- keeping their living space adequately tidy and attractive

7. Knowing how to be ASSERTIVE, you would see them:
- negotiating for their rights using a calm voice and logical argument
- willingly compromising more often than not
- standing up for the rights of people who are not able to fight their own battles

8. Having great EMOTIONAL CONTROL, you would see them:
- calmly doing relaxation exercises before any anxiety-provoking occasion such as an exam or interview
- controlling their temper in the face of frustration
- re-motivating themselves with rewards and positive self-talk when they hit a rough patch or a setback

Would it be a dream to live with such a creature? No, of course not. In fact, I think it would be a nightmare! You might appreciate it for an odd day or two, but not I guess for much longer. You wouldn't like to live with a paragon of consistent confident virtue anymore than they would like saints for their parents. So why did I ask you to visualize a teenager brimming with super confidence? Well, in self-development work I have found that even if our aim is to reach a *good-enough* standard 95% of the time, it is useful to have an image of perfection by which to judge our progress and inspire us to attain on the odd occasion!

About the Golden Rules

In the following chapter you will find the 21 Golden Rules for parents, which will show you step-by-step how to build a *good-enough* measure of inner and outer confidence in your teenager. Hopefully you will find the rules easy to remember so that they can be used as a day-to-day guide. As each rule contains a number of tips, I envisage that they could also serve as a checklist to consult when you encounter a problem that you feel overwhelmed by. I have devised the Golden Rules as 'standards of excellence' – reflecting on how you are measuring up against each Rule may give you an idea of where to start making some changes. But don't forget, as I said in my introduction, this is a 'rough guide' and not a 'bible'– it is good for parents, as well as teenagers, to break rules sometimes!

It is good for parents to break rules sometimes!

21 Golden Rules

Rule 1:
Teach by Example Before Giving Instructions

> 'I tell myself time and again to overlook mother's bad example. I only want to see her good points, and to look inside myself for what is lacking in her. But it doesn't work ...'
>
> Anne Frank, *Diary of a Young Girl*

It is no coincidence that I have put this particular rule at the top of my list. I firmly believe that the single most important thing we can do to help our teenagers develop confidence is to ensure that our own is as strong and healthy as it possibly can be. Ironically, it is during this stage of parenting that our own confidence is often at its most rocky. Not only is it usually midlife crisis time for us personally and in our careers, it is also a time when, as parents, we are continually faced with daunting dilemmas and decisions that we know will have profound consequences on the future of our child. Rarely can we be sure that we will get it right.

> *'Should we put our foot down now or will that make her more rebellious?'*
>
> *'I want him to be happy and enthusiastic about his work, but if I let him give up that subject, will it hold him back at University?'*

> *'If we ban smoking at home, won't that make them go underground with it and then what?'*

Once we have made up our agonized mind, we may then have to face a barrage of opposition. We can sometimes feel very isolated and alone. Even those closest to us may disagree with the line we take or the decision we make. Most of us find that over at least some issues we are on opposite sides of the fence to people who have hitherto been great sources of support and love. It's not just our newly empowered and often rebellious teens who will tell us that we are most definitely wrong. Many of the people who have consulted me have found that, at the same time, they also have to face opposition from their other children, their partner, the grandparents, teachers and sports coaches.

> 'Parents of young adolescents are often struggling with their own midlife crisis at the time when their children reach puberty.'
> Laurence Steinberg with Wendy Steinberg, *Crossing Paths*

Being human, many of us will then find that our frustration gets the better of us. We start responding to this criticism in ways that we know we shouldn't. For example, we might counter our teen's 'attack' with equally hurtful putdowns, such as *'That's a bit rare coming from someone with a pigsty of a bedroom like yours'* or an authoritarian reminder of the limit of their power, such as *'Don't cheek me or you'll be sorry'*.

Perhaps teaching by example will be the best parenting tool you will ever have. It is likely to continue to wield its impact long after our children have left home, as these examples from adults with confidence problems illustrate.

> Josie, a student from a small rural town, was in her first year at university in London – she was referred for counselling by her tutor who spotted that she was underachieving.

'My parents hardly ever went anywhere. We lived in a quiet street and although the neighbours were very friendly, mostly we kept ourselves to ourselves. Both mum and dad are quite shy – I suppose I take after them. Mum was on pills for her nerves from the doctors most of the time. She's not seriously ill or anything. She just gets very nervous and hasn't got much confidence.

... I never went on any of the school holidays – mum would have worried too much and anyway, I know I would have been too homesick. Our holidays were taken in our own caravan and we usually went to the same spot in Brittany. Often my mum's sister's family came with us.

I'm not complaining. I had a very happy childhood. We're a close family and I always got on well with my younger sister. She's my best friend.

It was a real culture shock when I came here to university. I'd only ever been to London once or twice before – just to do the usual visits to the museums. I didn't even have to come for an interview here.

... The girls in hall were very friendly; I suppose after a while I just retreated into my shell. I went out a few times but I felt silly – well, different, anyway. So I just started to make excuses.

But I don't want to go back home. I like the course and my parents would be really upset if I quit. You see, I'm the first in the family to go to university – it's funny, they think I'm really confident!'

Jill, a 37-year-old marketing manager, was seeking help because she was depressed.

'I never thought I'd hear myself saying this but I'm just like my mother – though she'd be the last person to see it. I'm everything she'd like to be. She's always telling me that she wished she had a life like mine. A busy job, always out meeting people and giving presentations. What she doesn't know is I hate it. I'm in a panic the whole time. I am always worrying about what people think of me.

And I know I am often considered "stand-offish". Boyfriends are always saying they can't get through to me. That's because I don't let them. The *truth is that I don't like myself very much – so basically I am like my mother. I can remember getting really mad with her as a teenager when she put herself down all the time. Now I find myself doing just the same. I may not be doing it openly like her, but inside I'm always knocking myself ... I don't think I've ever been truly happy.'*

Jim, a 29-year-old gas fitter, was dragged to counselling by his wife because their marriage was on the rocks, mainly due to his short fuse.

'My dad never stood up to my mother. She walked all over him. But then he never stood up to anyone ... I remember an occasion when we were on holiday when I was fourteen. We were on the beach and had set up our chairs and towels. We went off for a swim and when we came back the chairs had been moved and another family had taken our spot. My dad said nothing to them. When I said it wasn't fair, he just said (as he always did): "It's best not to make a fuss. It only leads to trouble."

I was determined no one was going get the better of me like that. But I don't want to blame him. I should be able to control myself ... it's all a front. You know, inside I'm a real softie. I don't want to hurt anyone. Would you believe what I really wanted to be was a doctor. I had the brains but not the bedside manner!

And you know this is my third attempt at the marriage game, don't you?'

All these parents had cared deeply for their children. There was never any shortage of love or security. But none of them were *good-enough* role models in terms of confidence. They would have been heart-broken if they knew what unhappiness this inadequacy had caused. Sadly, it would have been so easy to correct. It is never too late to build confidence.

So for those of you who know that your own confidence is shakier than you would like it to be, here are some tips which I hope will help.

It is never too late to become a confident parent.

Top Tips

- **Find sources of support before you need them**. Ironically, the worst time to be searching for support is when our self-esteem is at its rockiest. If you know that there is a chance that your confidence could plummet under the pressure of parenting your teen, make sure that you have already identified the people to whom you could turn to for help. This could be a professional person such as your doctor, or an approachable teacher at school. Tell them of your concern. (Your lack of confidence may not be obvious to the outside world.) Ask them if they would be prepared to support you through any crisis. You could even talk through some contingency plans with them. To save you worrying alone with some of your worst fears, make plans for how to cope should your worst fear be realized. Preparation is one of the unsung skills of confident people.

  Test yourself with these examples:

  - Your daughter is sleeping with her boyfriend. What would you do if she became pregnant? Who would you first turn to? What organizations might be your best support?

  - Your son is going around with a group of friends and you know that at least two of his friends smoke cannabis. What would you do if the police come knocking on the door one day? Who could best advise you in this situation?

  - Your daughter fails an important exam. She is devastated and won't be consoled by you? Who could you turn to for support?

  - Your son's girlfriend has finished with him. He says he doesn't care, but he's become very moody. He isn't washing or eating very much. You are worried he might be becoming seriously depressed. Who could you turn to? Who might be the best person to talk to your son?

Preparation is one of the unsung skills of confident people.

- **Meet regularly with other parents of teens** – even though you may moan and groan together sometimes, make sure that the majority of your contacts enjoy being parents most of the time. You can either do this informally with friends or neighbours, or formally by joining a parenting network group. (Your library or the Internet will have details of groups in your area.) The test of whether a group or friends are truly supportive of you is whether you can feel free to share your successes as well as your problems. Try it out by telling someone how pleased you were with a good decision you made or how well you responded in a certain crisis. (Tough medicine, I know, for people who lack confidence!)

- **Start and finish each day doing something that you enjoy**. How many times do you go to bed feeling stressed and harassed and then wake-up feeling even worse? Get in the habit of making both getting up and going to bed relaxing and self-nurturing experiences. Try taking an aromatherapy bath instead of a shower; listening to your favourite music instead of the depressing news; reading a chapter of an uplifting novel before reading the paper, or pampering your body with luxurious creams before 'throwing on' your clothes in the morning.

- **Start a new learning activity**. Have you ever glanced at your teens' homework or curriculum and felt woefully aware of how out-of-date some of your education and skills have become? (And, yes, they do rub it in!) Try counteracting the depressing effect of this reality by learning something new. This should be a stretching activity, but an enjoyable one. (You have enough of the daunting kind of challenges in your everyday life!)

> 'Oh, to be only half as wonderful as my child thought I was when he was small, and only half as stupid as my teenager now thinks I am.'
>
> Rebecca Richards

- **Don't ignore your own emotional hurts** – you can expect plenty during this time from your teenager. By this age he or she should know the tender spots on your Achilles heel. And, unless they are unusually saintly, they will attack you there either because you will not give them what they want or simply because they have some axe to grind with the outside world. Our confidence can never be solid while we have emotional wounds festering inside us. Get into the habit of giving yourself a small treat or getting some extra support as soon as you can after you have been hurt. For example, if you get put down for being your age, immediately ring a good friend who you know will give you some sympathy. Or, should 90% of the meal you spent an hour preparing get left without comment, treat yourself to a 20-minute break listening to *your* favourite CD.

Your confidence will be even more vulnerable to these kinds of hurts if you are harbouring emotional wounds from other sources as well. For example, we are less likely to stay strong in the face of a taunt or rejection from our teenager if we are still smarting from a quarrel with our partner or disappointment at work, or indeed the put-downs we ourselves received in our teens. If you suspect that this area is a particularly difficult one for you, try my book or audio tape *Emotional Confidence*, which could help.

- **Make time to continue doing an activity that you are good at**. In spite of the fact that our teens often seem to be strangers passing in the night, looking after them is still incredibly time-consuming. It is so tempting to give up our free time to running a taxi service for them or because we are tired, just vegetating in front of the telly. Make the time to carry on doing at least one leisure activity which boosts your confidence simply because you *know* you are good at it. This will counteract the effect of having to live in the uncomfortable state of not knowing whether you are doing the right thing by your teen or not. (Aren't we so often working for long-term benefits in an atmosphere of short-term angst?!)

- **Join an Assertiveness Training or Confidence Building class**. I can't tell you how often I have worked with parents of teens on such courses. Not only will they give you ideas on how to cope and techniques to help you stand up for your rights, I can assure you that you will also have fun and make long-lasting friendships.

Rule 2:
Ensure Your Wisdom is One
(But Only One) Step Ahead

Adolescence is a time when human brains and bodies go through important phases in their growth. Teenagers begin to develop the ability to think more broadly and deeply. The world that they perceive is much more complex than he or she has yet experienced, and the choices it offers (like ours!) no longer appear simple. The lists of available options are bewilderingly endless. Additionally, this is also the time when academic pressure is hotting up; curricula are more seriously challenging and teenagers are being exposed to a wider range of ideas, people and cultures.

Not surprisingly, therefore, teenagers feel more secure if they think that they can rely on at least one parent to be a reliable source of wisdom on the issues which are of central concern to them and their development at this age.

But of course, I am not suggesting that you need a degree in adolescent development before you start parenting a teen! On the contrary, be assured that a 'know-all' parent can be severely damaging to fragile confidence. Children of any age must never feel outclassed by our 'superior' adult knowledge or feel that their behaviour, progress or health concerns are merely being judged as typical or atypical of a certain theory or set of statistics on adolescence.

> 'I didn't want to hear about "typical adolescent problems" or "other girls" or "you'll grow out of it". I didn't want to be treated the same as all-the-other-girls but as Anne in her own right.'
>
> Anne Frank

I am convinced that parents who do have some forewarning of what they and their children might expect during the teen years do cope better and are able to be more supportive to their children. During the course of reading this book, you should pick up most of the crucial 'basics' in terms of confidence building, but there are some other areas of knowledge that I believe would also be helpful to explore.

In the following Top Tips list I have inserted some questions to ask yourself and discuss with your partner or friends. I haven't included any answers for two reasons. Firstly, they would probably be out-of-date by the time this book is even printed. Secondly, I am hoping that this book is going to be read by parents from many different countries and cultures around the world and many of the answers could be different for each one of these.

If the questions raise some doubts in your mind (or cause a few heated arguments at home!), this is a sure sign that you may need to do some homework yourself. In my *Further Help* section at the end of the book, I have recommended several good books and Internet sites, which could help. Alternatively, your local youth service or school should be more than happy to advise you. You may also find some of the answers by looking in teenage magazines, or watching their programmes on TV, or picking the brains of friends or relatives.

But don't forget that the key to living up to this rule (or any other for that matter) is humility! In this field *no one* can claim to be an expert for long. It is all too easy to become out-of-date. The lifestyles of teenagers and the issues which concern them change fast and furiously. What was a priority for one child may no longer be relevant for the generation which is only a couple of years behind. Your first child could sail through puberty without an apparent care in the world, while your next child could start exhibiting every symptom of adolescent ailment known to medical mankind. Alternatively, one child could have discovered their true vocation at the age of six, while the next appears to need 24-hour career counselling.

Even if we were blessed with perfect parents ourselves, or have already successfully reared six teens or obtained a distinction in 'Adolescent Studies', we cannot assume we ever know enough. Every one of us could do with checking from time to time that our wisdom is still good-enough to underpin the developing confidence of our teenagers.

Check that you know enough about the issues that are important to your teen to underpin their developing confidence.

Top Tips

- **Swot up on your knowledge of adolescent development** – it will help you to know what physical and mental changes you can expect to take place during these years of growth. You should be able to explain to them what is going on in their body and how that might be affecting their health, feelings and behaviour.
  - Do you know what is now the typical age for puberty for girls and boys?
  - Do you know at what age, roughly, you can expect a boy's voice to break?
  - Do you know at what age most teenagers start experimenting with sex?
  - What are the differences between the physical growth and emotional maturity patterns of boys and girls at this age?

■ **Increase your awareness of teenage culture** – it will help
if you have a good knowledge of the *current* concerns and
preoccupations of this age group. If you understand these you will
be less likely to jump to your own conclusions based just on *your*
own personal experience or prejudice.
  – Do you know what is at the top of most teenagers' list of
    worries?
  – Do most teenagers worry about their weight nowadays – or is
    the media concern about eating disorders quite out of
    proportion in the light of the latest research?
  – Do you know if peer pressure to smoke or take drugs is stronger
    than average in your community?

■ **Talk to as wide a range of parents of teenagers as you
can** – it helps to have an idea of the experiences and problems
which families outside your own immediate circle of friends
commonly encounter. It may help reduce unnecessary worry and
prevent some molehills from becoming mountainous quarrels.
Joining a parenting class, workshop, support group or Internet
chat-site can all be good ways of doing this. (You may also pick up
many handy coping hints in the process!)
  – Can you name the three commonest causes of conflict between
    parents and teenagers in your country?
  – What is the average mid-week bedtime time for 14-year-olds
    and 17-year-olds in your community?

■ **Acquire a professional assessment of their individual
intellect and skills**. It is obviously important to have an
objective opinion of their innate potential. But it is also
important, in terms of confidence building, to know how likely it
is that they will be able to realize this, given the current standards
and opportunities in their school and community and the trade
in which they wish to work. This will help you to help them set
realistic goals. You may be able to get this kind of assessment
through the school, but many parents are now having their
children privately assessed by educational psychologists or career

advisors. Many of these offer reduced fees for people on low incomes.

- What are the current necessary academic qualifications of people training for a) accountancy b) website design c) music d) nursing, or any other career which they may be currently considering?
- Which are the three top social and personal skills that employers today value most?
- What is the difference between IQ, EQ and SQ and can, or should, these and other kinds of intelligence be tested and assessed?

- **Find out which are the common telltale signs of physical and mental health problems in this age group** – this will help to avoid crises and unnecessary worry. It will also give you an idea of when you should give them a 'gentle push' to face up to a symptom which may need professional help.
  - How might you tell the difference between a pre-exam tension headache and one which you should consult a doctor about?
  - How would you tell whether the proverbial obsession with zits has become a case for 'acne action'?
  - If their sporting activity has decreased and you notice they become breathless more easily, what other problem might you be on the look out for as well?
  - If a sore throat has persisted for more than 14 days, should you ask for a blood test for glandular fever?
  - Is it common for girls to miss periods in the months leading up to exams?
  - Is skipping meals a possible sign of bulimia or anorexia?
  - If the pupils of their eyes are constantly dilated, what could be causing this symptom?
  - If they are reporting sleeplessness, what should concern you most – early morning waking or difficulty in getting off to sleep?

■ **Gather information about community resources** – you
should have this handy even if you think you may never need it.
(Just think how confidence boosting it could be for your teenager
to give this helpful information to a friend?)
– Do you know the number of your local drugs help-line?
– Does your school have a free counselling service?
– Do you have the address of your local youth advisory service?
– Do you know of any charities who might be able to help
  low-income families with grants for school trips, extra tuition
  for learning problems, adventure holidays or sports coaching?
– Do you know of any organizations which counsel or advise
  families going through divorce?
– Do you know the address of your local bereavement counselling
  service?

'My adolescent problems took their most violent form in a shyness
of a pathological degree. Few people realize, now, that I have always
been ... an extremely shy creature – I compensate for this shyness by
the typical Williams heartiness and bluster and sometimes explosive
fury of behaviour.'

Tennessee Williams

Rule 3:
Listen Three Times as Much as you Talk

'If I had to pick a single suggestion that was designed to help virtually all relationship and family problems, it would be to become a better listener ... becoming a better listener is an art form, yet it's not at all complicated.'

Richard Carlson, *Don't Sweat the Small Stuff with Your Family*

I hope you won't take this rule literally! I am not suggesting that you do a time-analysis of every conversation you have with your teen. But I do hope that you will take the point that, for the purpose of confidence building, the apparently passive activity of listening is vital.

Why is listening so important?

Firstly, it is one of the most effective ways of showing a teenager respect and feeding their self-esteem. This is the main reason why every counsellor and psychotherapist spends so long refining this skill.

Attentive listening is an effective way of showing a teenager respect and feeding their self-esteem.

Secondly, attentive listening is one of the fastest ways of getting to know a person. And don't forget that although you may think you know your child through and through after 12 years of intimate life with them, during these crucial developmental years most parents find themselves regularly surprised. With all the extra activity within their bodies and the extra input from the outside world, teenagers are in a state of permanent change. This means that our knowledge of them needs to be continually updated.

Thirdly, talking to a *good* listener about ourselves – our thoughts and ideas – is the most effective way of clarifying what we need and want out of life. It is infinitely more useful than seeking direct advice.

Undoubtedly, some people seem to be blessed from birth with a gift to listen. In fact, most people who apply to do counselling courses name this skill as one of their natural strengths. I certainly remember doing so and I also remember being seriously disappointed to find out during the course just how bad a listener I really was! Most of the time I was actually hearing what I wanted or expected to hear. It took months and months of rigorous and confrontational practical work to change some of my bad habits. (Even now, 25 years later, they re-surface from time to time, especially when I am over-stressed or emotionally involved.)

As a parent you won't of course need the level of skill you would expect from a counsellor. But listening is such a key confidence-building tool that I am sure it would be worthwhile reading through the following guidelines. You could re-read them whenever you find yourself locked in communication problems with your teen (and who doesn't at some time!) For those of you who have shy, nervous or inarticulate children it might well be worthwhile to find a friend with whom to test out some of the strategies that I suggest. Good listening is not a skill that can be learned theoretically. It takes practise and good feedback to develop.

Top Tips

- **Avoid directly suggesting you want or need 'a talk'** – however kind your tone or however much they may need to talk, when the idea is put in that way it is often perceived at worst as 'a threat' and at best 'a bore'.

- **Pick your moment and location carefully** – of course the perfect time will rarely be available, but at least try to choose a time when neither of you is too stressed, tired or itching to focus your attention elsewhere. With boys, especially, it is usually best to talk while doing something together or alongside each other.

  As a general rule, it is best to avoid public situations, particularly for heart-to-heart talks or resolving conflict. However, I can recall having very meaningful and memorable conversations with my daughters in cafes while out shopping together. Perhaps the closeness we felt as a result of doing a shared 'girly' fun activity helped create the right atmosphere and allowed one of us to seize the moment.

Some people find that it is much easier for their teen to open up when they are in their own territory. Others have told me that they have found that bedrooms are the biggest 'no-go' area for conversations.

So once again, it is down to trial and error with each and every individual child.

- **Stay patient and positive**. As long as you keep in mind that privacy is a major concern for this age group, and you are prepared to be rebuffed innumerable times and seize moments which may not be ideal for you, you will **eventually win through**. The temptation to talk to someone who **really wants to *listen*** is one very few humans can resist for long!

- **Go easy on the questions** – instead use statements, observations and self-disclosure. You can say, for example: *'I noticed that you didn't eat your breakfast this morning. Perhaps you just weren't hungry. I know I never felt like eating just before an exam.'* (Rather than: *'Why didn't you eat your breakfast? ... Are you worried about the exam?'*)

Even if you don't elicit a response, at least you have shown that you care and understand their feelings.

■ **Mentally gag yourself for the first minute or two of your talk** – don't interrupt with your own thoughts, feelings or shared experiences. This is much harder to do than you might think. We often interrupt with our own story or feeling or experience quite automatically. (*'Funny you should say that, I was also ...'* / *'That never happens to me, I always ...'*) This is fine if you are having an ordinary social conversation with two adults, but less helpful if you are an adult with more power, articulacy and experience than a young person with fledgling confidence.

■ **Use body language or encouraging 'noises' to show that you are listening** – having gagged yourself, don't turn to stone! It is important to communicate in some way that you *really are* listening. You can do this by, for example:
  – stopping or slowing down what you are doing
  – nodding
  – opening your eyes a *little* wider (not too much direct eye contact – it embarrasses and threatens most self-conscious adolescents)
  – leaning forward a little
  – uttering the *odd* 'mnhs', 'Ohs', 'Ahs' or 'Really's!'
  – smiling (appropriately and not patronizingly, of course!)

■ **If they dry up, resist the temptation to comment or speak for them** – by coming in with your view or interpretation of what they are trying to say. (Yes, you *will* do it unless you consciously put the brakes on yourself!)

■ **Reflect back what you have heard** – you could just repeat some of the words or phrases they have used or the last sentence. This may seem a very strange thing to do until you have tried it. In fact, it is a common listening technique used by all the professionals. Watch a good chat show host or good coach and you will see how it works. For example:

Teen:	*Well, of course I'm pissed off ... I saw Sarah today coming out of school, didn't I?*
You:	*Sarah?*
Teen:	*Yeah, and she just walked straight past me.*
You:	*She didn't say anything to you?*
Teen:	*Yeah ... last Saturday we were supposed to be going to the gig together. She said she'd be in the club that evening ... like a real wally, I waited three hours for her.*
You:	*Three hours!*

- **Try to feel what they might be feeling** – sharing your own possible emotional reactions as if you were in their shoes sometimes helps them to express theirs more clearly. For example: *'I guess you were pretty upset.' / 'I think I'd have been boiling mad.'*

- **Tune in to their body language** – but don't copy it exactly. If they are casually sitting down, sit down too, but you don't have to put your feet on the table as well! Similarly, if they are talking loudly you don't have to shout but at least don't whisper.

- **Check out that you are picking up the right clues** – teenagers are not usually as articulate as we are, so noticing their body language is very important. With boys who tend to be less emotionally articulate than girls in many cultures, this can help them express feelings they may not even know they had. You can say, for example:
  'I notice you tapping your finger ... I was wondering if I am irritating you'
  or,
  'I saw you glance at your watch, are you in a hurry or do you feel we have just been going over old stuff again?'

- **Stay comfortable with silences** – they may need longer than you would need to think of what to say or summon up the courage to speak honestly. Use the silences to pick up feelings and observe body language – you will still be listening.

■ **To get them back on track, refer to phrases or words**
   ***they* have used** – rather than directly telling them that they
   have digressed. For example:

   You: *'When you said just now you met her coming out of school, were*
            you on your own?'

   Teen: *'No, there was a whole crowd of us ... and that git Kevin started*
            having a go at me ... He ...'.

■ **Summarize what you *think* they have said** – do this from
   time to time and always at the end of important conversations. For
   example:

   'Hang on a minute, can I just check what I think you said? You're still
   being bullied but you don't want us to do anything about it.'

■ **Use a metaphor or another example to clarify your**
   understanding – use one which seems to sum up the essence
   of the message which you think that they are trying to convey.
   Obviously it should be one which is meaningful for them. For
   example:

   'Sounds as though it feels a bit like standing in goal with a blindfold on'
   or,

   'Was it a bit like that day when we got back from the sales having spent
   all day buying things that didn't really fit us?'

■ **Ask 'open questions' to encourage more than one-word**
   answers – for example, use questions which start with *what, why*
   and *how.*

■ **Use 'closed questions' to round up your talk** – these will
   usually do the opposite of the open questions. They encourage
   one-word answers. For example:

   'Do you just want to forget it now?... So shall we both get to bed?' or *'Do*
   you think I understand more now?' or *'Have we covered everything now?'*

■ **Move back or stand up when you want to finish** – most
   people find themselves doing this naturally the moment they
   think they want to end a conversation. But in my experience

many people do not, so it is worth checking yourself. It is one of those natural body signals that we can consciously use to influence the outcome we want. It can be more effective than trying to interrupt a teenager on a mission to convert you to his or her point of view!

- **Say what you intend to do or think about as a result of listening to them** – this will really boost their confidence because it will indicate that you have taken what they said very seriously. For example:
  'Well, I think I understand now what is going on. I'd like to talk this over with mum before I say yes.'
  'I can see now that all my questioning when you come home feels pressurizing. I'll try to curb my nosiness.'
  'I'll ring the school to make an appointment to see Mr Duncan tomorrow.'

- **Give them a compliment** – this must be sincere, of course. If possible give them specific feedback so they will know exactly what they did well. For example: *'I know it must have been difficult to tell me ... I admire you for having the courage to ...' / 'I think you explained the situation very clearly.'*

- **Finish with a positive comment** – this could be sharing a feeling or summarizing what your talk together seems to have achieved. For example: *'I really enjoyed hearing about ... ' / 'It seems as though we have cleared the air – I'm pleased.'*

Rule 4:
Think Before You Speak

'The turning point for me was the day that I heard my mother's words coming out of my own mouth.'

parent in counselling

It is so easy to verbally put our foot in it with teenagers. Firstly, it is during their teen years that most children start, quite literally, to speak a different language. You will notice that they are using words and phrases that either you have never heard of or you have never heard used in that context. (It would be pointless for me to give you examples now because they would be out-of-date next week. Anyway, you will experience the phenomena very soon yourself!)

The way forward for better communication is not for you to start using their new language (as well-meaning parents often try to do). That's the fast track to losing their respect – they will perceive you as being either patronizing or just plain silly. Also, they might well become annoyed with you because you are undermining something that they need to do. Their use of this new language (and laughing at

your 'antiquated' expressions!) is an important way of differentiating themselves from you and your generation. Using it helps them to be accepted by their peers. Your challenge as a parent is to stay yourself without sounding like an unapproachable relic from the ark!

Secondly, this is a time when we might well start to use more unhelpful 'auto-language'. This is the expression I use to refer to the words and phrases which come out of our mouths without our conscious consent! They are programmed responses, many of which we picked up in early childhood. The teenage years are a time when 'Like mother, like daughter' and 'Like father, like son' syndromes emerge in us in full force. You may have already heard your parent's voice resounding through your own, possibly saying things to your children you always vowed you'd never say. This can be a very un-comfortable and disconcerting experience. Very few people whose confidence was dented by their own parents' words want to inflict the same experience on their children. Most of us try very hard to do the exact opposite. But, unless you opt for a complete 'brain-wash', you are stuck for life with many of your auto-language responses. They were programmed into your brain at an early age and are therefore exceptionally hard to shift. There is always a danger that they will emerge, in spite of your 'better self', when you are highly stressed, over-tired or emotionally wounded. As all of these states are familiar to parents of teens, is it any wonder that you may sound more like *your* mum and dad during these years?!

But let's not forget that not all our unwanted auto-language is inherited from our parents. We also pick up phrases and sayings that are commonly used in our surrounding culture. Many of these are relics from an age when 'children were seen but not heard'. Because they are part of everyday language we may not notice when we are using them. Confident teenagers will dismiss them and make fun of them, but the not-so confident ones are at risk of being hurt by them.

But, let's not despair too much. We still have a conscious mind and it can help us exert a great deal of control over the language we use.

**The key to good communication is to stay
yourself without sounding like an unapproachable
relic from the ark!**

Top Tips

- **Play for time whenever you feel emotionally charged** –
this will help you to think before you speak. Before having any
serious conversation with your teen, try to make a habit of taking
time to de-stress yourself (see Rule 15 for tips on how to do this)
and prepare what you are going to say.

- **Keep it short and keep it simple** – this is a tip taken straight
from the mouths of all the leading communication gurus. The less
'flowery' your language, the less of those alienating and
antiquated expressions you are likely to use.

- **Make a 'black list'** – write down the phrases that you heard
your parents or teachers using that you want to avoid repeating.
Add any unwanted clichés you may have picked up from living in
the culture in which you grew up. Read through this list
frequently for a month. This will fix the phrases in your conscious
mind and you will become much more aware of when you are
using them. If this doesn't work, try showing the list to your teen
and ask them to tell you when you use them. They will usually be
more than happy to oblige!

- **Avoid using 'age labels'** – I certainly know I don't like being
lumped together with all 'the middle-aged' people in the world.
But I know that I am still guilty of committing this 'sin' myself.
(And yes, in a sense I have been doing it all the time throughout
this book!)
  But in face-to-face communication, I believe we should all
make a conscious effort to try to avoid using these kinds of labels
(direct or implied). They do little good for anyone's self-esteem. So
watch out for expressions, such as:

'You teens ...'
'Your generation are ...'
'Just typical adolescent behaviour ... '
'You boys and your macho ...'
'Girls of your age today are just ...'
'It's the hormones again!'
'You and your friends, you're all the same ...'
'Act your age ...'
'When you are our age you'll realize ...'
'You think you're so grown up but ...'
'You may be a teenager but ...'

- **Watch out for 'tit for tat' responses to exaggerations** –
  teenagers are, of course, prone to using these. It is understandable
  that they will do so. Their emotions are so often on the boil and
  they frequently feel very insecure and powerless. Here are some
  examples:
  'Everything is a mess'
  'No-one ever listens to me'
  This is the only chance I'll ever get'
  'I'll die if she doesn't come'
  'You always say ...'
  'Everyone else's mother let's them'
  'I can't go in without it, he'll crucify me'
  'My hair is a complete mess!'

It is also understandable that even the most rational, articulate
parents often respond with similarly over-blown words and
phrases. After all, we are also frequently feeling powerless and
frustrated! When our brains pick up these emotive language cues
either our hurt inner child or our controlling 'auto-parent' have a
tendency to leap into similar action without our consent. As a
result, you may (like the best of us!), find yourself using
overstatements without even realizing that you are doing so. Ask
your nearest and dearest to tell you when you say something like:

'All you ever think about is you'
'You are driving me to complete distraction'
'How can you say that when we've sacrificed everything so that you could ...'
'Your mother never has a moment to herself, leave her alone'
'Your father will have a heart attack if he finds out ...'

- **Cut, apologize for and rephrase the negative clichés** – we all laugh at them when we hear them in sitcoms, but they are not so funny in real-life. They are one of the worst kind of put-downs. Their sarcasm cuts into self-esteem even if they are rapidly thrown back in our face (where indeed they deserve to be). And yet they get used generation after generation with very little modification.

  Now that we live in an age which is more aware of the power of conditioning, we can stop the cycle. But you will find it hard, as indeed I did. Often the best we can hope for is that when we hear ourselves say them, we stop, say sorry and rephrase what we wanted to say. For example:

  'Is this what you call early? ... Oh, sorry, that was unnecessarily sarcastic ... Seriously, I have been very worried about you. You said you would be in early and I assumed that meant before 11.30.'
  'One day you'll be sorry ... the way you carry on, you'll become a ... Oh God, I sound like my father ... sorry, that wasn't very helpful, I was just sounding off because I am worried.'
  'So, that's in fashion, is it? ... Sorry, that's a put-down. I was a bit taken aback, it looks odd to me, but then I am over 40!'
  'Oh, I see, that's tidy – I didn't realize ... Sorry I shouldn't be sarcastic. I know you have tidied it, but you have forgotten to remove the coffee mugs and your boots and coat are still on the chair.'

> 'Whenever I come sailing in with a new hairstyle, I can read the disapproval on their faces, and I can be sure someone will ask what film star I'm trying to imitate. My reply that it is my own invention is greeted with cynicism.'
>
> Anne Frank

Rule 5:
Review the 'Rulebook' Jointly and Frequently

> 'The joy of being young is to disobey – but the trouble is, there are no longer any orders.'
>
> Jean Cocteau

Of course no self-respecting teen loves rules. Indeed, an essential part of their growing-up job is to hate them and break them!

Perhaps you feel that your child has been doing just this from the moment he or she could walk or talk! If so, you may well wonder why rules should suddenly become such a special 'issue' at this time. The reason is that during their teen years, testing them takes on some different and quite specific extra functions.

In their earlier years, children test rules either to get more attention from those who care for them or to establish a sense of security. 'Pushing the limits' gives them the confirmation that they are still being seen and heard and it helps them to map out their safety zones. It is a way of finding out where they can go and what they can say without getting hurt or losing the love of their carers.

The moral implications of rules pass younger children by. This is quite simply because it isn't until adolescence that our brains develop their capacity for abstract reasoning. So, until this time most children do not have the neural equipment to allow them to grapple with intellectual concepts. This means that although they may *know* what the world thinks is right and wrong, they cannot understand *why* they should or shouldn't do something. Once they reach teenhood, testing the 'rulebook' becomes a tool which they can use to explore moral ideas and beliefs. (Provoking you into argument is of course another popular way of doing the same thing!)

Discovering their own belief system is part of the quest for self-knowledge. (Self-knowledge is one of the essential elements of inner confidence, which we discussed earlier. See page 5.) Teenagers naturally experience an urge to find out what kind of person they are or want to be and to establish their own set of consistent values and beliefs. If they complete this task, they will then be able to act quickly and decisively on their own. In contrast, children who don't discover their own belief system will always be dependent on others to help them make difficult decisions and let them know what is a right and what is a wrong course of action to take.

Furthermore, not only do children need to challenge the rulebook in order to firm up their inner confidence, they need to do so for their outer confidence as well! If our children were to become the acquiescent saints that we sometimes wish they would be, how would they learn the invaluable skills of debate, negotiation, assertiveness and emotional control?

These are, after all, essentially practical skills and they cannot be learned effectively in a theoretical way. Teenagers need to use a hands-on experimental approach – with you, the parents, as the ideal guinea pigs! You are the close-at-hand authority figures and have already proved your unconditional love innumerable times before.

There is no escaping the challenges of the 'rulebook' if you truly want a confident teen!

Of course it is tempting to try and avoid the trials and tribulations that obviously result from working through this particular stage of development. Many parents would say that their lives are difficult enough without having to turn their home into a battleground of wills. So it is not surprising that they opt out by, for example, doing one of the following:

- throwing away the rulebook: *'Okay, it's your life ... you make a mess of it if you want to ... I don't mind ... you'll soon find out on your own ... I don't know what's right or wrong these days ... you've got a key, do what you like ...'*
- handing over the task to someone else: *'Wait till your father gets home ... I wonder what your teacher is going to say when I tell him ... I didn't make the rules ... it's the law – a matter for the police ... God is your judge, not me ...'*

   – taking a 'sickie': *'My head's hurting, I can't argue ... you'll kill me if you carry on like this ... I'm too stressed ...'*

Hopefully, you haven't yet succumbed to the temptation of going down one or other of these routes. Establishing and enforcing rules and boundaries are very much part of our parental responsibilities. Confidence cannot be built in an environment without them. It would be too scary and too risky. A light scorching of fingers can be informative and 'character building', but burning them can be discouraging and possibly dangerous. For example, if a teenage boy gets really drunk the night before a football match – and consequently plays badly – this can teach him an important lesson about the effects of alcohol abuse, whereas if a teenager secretly raids the forbidden drinks cabinet for 'Dutch courage' before driving, this could have dangerous consequences. Similarly, if a 13-year-old girl stays up most of the night listening to music and gets a late mark as a result, this can teach her a lesson about being more responsible, but if a 16-year-old girl skips the 'curfew' for an all night party before a crucial exam, this could have discouraging consequences for later years.

I cannot guarantee that reviewing the rulebook frequently with your teen will dramatically reduce the hassles associated with this important parental task. But it will certainly help your child develop confidence in the process – and that has to be some kind of compensation! And looking ahead, another reassuring fact to keep in mind is that research has shown that the more young people are involved in this kind of decision making, the more likely they are to develop the same attitudes as their parents in late adolescence.

> 'By slowly making your house rules more flexible, you give your teenager both freedom and safe limits ... so the goal is not to abandon the playpen altogether but to gradually enlarge it.'
>
> Steve Chalke, *The Parentalk Guide to the Teenage Years*

Top Tips

■ **Clarify your own values** – do this on your own or with your co-parent or friends before you enter any discussion with your teen. You need to clarify in your own mind which rules are non-negotiable. These will be the ones which protect and support the core values and principles by which you want to lead your life and bring up your family.

Why not test yourself *now* by listing:

– 3 non-negotiable values or principles which you would expect anyone with whom you lived to respect (for example, non-violence, loyalty and honesty)
– 6 values which you would ideally like to be respected, but which would be open to some negotiation (for example, privacy, self-direction and cleanliness).

Once you have done this, set aside some time to talk to your teenager. You could begin by talking about the list you have just made and then asking for their opinion on it. Alternatively, you might prefer to look out for an informal way of bringing up the subject, such as after watching the news or a T.' soap together, where there is an example of someone standing up for their values, or a person flouting someone else's. Either way, it is important to eventually steer the discussion in a direction which will help them to think about their core values as well.

When you are looking at the rules or discussing issues which relate to them, you can refer back to these discussions. Any imposed restriction will be much more acceptable if it is seen to be in line with either your own non-negotiable values or their own values. For example:

'I know that you are not always hungry at the same time as us, but do you remember when we talked about this on the way to town last month? I explained why I felt so strongly that it should be one of our family rules that we all sit down for a meal together at least three or four times each week. This seems to be the best way for us to keep up with each others' lives. It's very important to me that we don't become

strangers that pass in the hall. It can so easily happen now that you are all growing up and are understandably out so much.'

'I appreciate that you do not like doing the washing-up, but I remember when we were talking about values last week – you were saying that justice was a key one for you ... that's why we agreed to have a rota.'

- **Don't beat about the bush** – *'Call a spade a spade'* as they say in Yorkshire, where I lived for much of my adulthood. Don't be shy of the word 'rule'. Don't skirt around the subject. Be clear that a rule is what it is. It means that certain behaviour is unacceptable, rather than just merely disliked.

  Don't ever assume that because 'everyone' knows that you have 'strong views' on a certain subject, they will automatically know that there is an unwritten rule.

  For example, if your teenager knows full well that you don't like smoking or swearing, don't assume that means that they know that they or their friends are not allowed to smoke or swear in the house.

  Similarly, they may know how seriously you view their academic work and how strongly you feel about the importance of homework. They may even respect you for your concern and fully agree with you. But, you may still need to clearly establish that one of the house rules is that homework is to be completed every night before starting any social activity. So instead of saying, *'I can't believe you didn't do your homework before going out when you know how important it is'*, you could try saying something like, *'We both believe that your academic work has to have top priority at the moment. Can we agree that doing your homework before coming down to watch TV is one of our rules?'*

- **Check in advance that you both know what the penalties are for breaking the rules** – don't find yourself in the position of trying to think these up in the heat of the aftermath. Aim at trying to get their agreement to the penalty whenever you can. For example:

'So, we agree that you will be in by 10 pm on weekdays and that if you are not you will forfeit your right to stay out till midnight on Saturdays.'

- **Choose a time when you are both positive and relaxed to do your reviews** – as I write this, I can hear imaginary voices laughing derisively at this suggestion! Of course times like these are rare at your stage of family life, but at least you can try not to do the opposite! Refuse to get into a discussion about rules in the middle of an argument or late at night when your energy levels are low. If your teen tries to provoke you into an argument on the subject at an inappropriate time (and they will!), keep calm and repeatedly suggest a time when you would be able and willing to talk. For example:

  'I appreciate you think you have done your fair share, but I don't want to discuss the cleaning rota now – we're both het up and tired. Let's talk about it over a coffee when you come in from school tomorrow. I'll make sure I'm back early.'

- **Demonstrate your willingness to bend the rules occasionally** – but only on an advance notice basis and if they come prepared with a good argument to back up their case. It will give their confidence a terrific boost if they feel they can sometimes make you relax the rulebook. For example:
'So you feel it is a special occasion and you have been working really hard without a break for two weeks ... I suppose you have a point. Let's say tonight's an exception then.'

But don't always expect the favour to be returned. This is a game about power and don't forget that its cards are heavily stacked in your favour most of the time.

'I remember being let off our chores during exam times – this was really good 'cos it showed mum and dad were really focused on us and our needs.'

young adult

'We were too over-confident about bringing up our fourth child. Our biggest mistake was to relax, having coasted rather easily with the first three. She needed firmer boundaries than the others. After one scary near-miss incident we talked and talked and established new ground-rules. Things improved gradually over the next six months without any pressure from us.'

parent (now leader of a parent support group)

Rule 6:
Aim to Strike a Deal in 90% of Your Conflicts

'Conflict, although painful, can be the cutting edge of learning and growth – sometimes out of the breakdown of communication comes breakthrough.'

Sheila Munroe, *Communicating with Your Teenager*

However careful you are to make sure the rulebook is jointly agreed, there will always be some (or a great deal!) of conflict to resolve. In fact, I believe that it is impossible for any group of truly confident people to live under one roof without conflict. How can it be otherwise, when each person is so much an individual and everyone is fervently convinced that they have a right to stand up for their own particular beliefs and needs?

So, first and foremost it is important to accept that you are going to live in an argumentative atmosphere for some years to come.

Secondly, it is equally important to try to view this inevitability in a positive light. A good argument, after all, *can* be great fun and very stimulating. (Ask any member of the British parliament!) Most successful confident people whom I have met seize opportunities for a good debate. They know the value of well-managed conflict. They are not frightened by it because they have experienced how it can stretch their potential and encourage creative solutions to problems that could never have emerged without it. Even when the debate results in a 'beg to differ' resolution, if it has been well-managed, it often increases mutual respect and bonds participants more closely together. An interesting example of this is when a political minister retires and often he or she is praised by their political opponents. It is obvious that their opponents not only enjoyed the sparring over the parliamentary benches, they also admired them for standing up for what they believed in and were even able to maintain a personal friendship with them as well.

Of course there will be moments during or after conflict when you will feel quite low and despairing, but once you have given yourself a recuperative rest, aim to return to a positive attitude. Even if your child is not destined to enter into such an obviously conflict-laden lifestyle as politics, I am sure that you would want them to become the kind of adult who can confidently handle other kinds of life-battles and emerge with his or her respect intact. One way of ensuring that they will be able to do this is to give them plenty of negotiating experience. I hope these tips may also help you to improve your role-modelling of this tricky art!

Top tips
- **Before you negotiate:**
  - Think about your absolute 'bottom line' position – you may need to think about standing by your core values and principles. You also need to be clear about what you, or they, can reasonably afford to lose.
  - Remind yourself (and later make it clear to your teen) that negotiating is about achieving a Win/Win outcome – neither party should feel like a loser at the end.
  - Accept that this is not a negotiation between two equals. You have more power. You will need to make allowances (without patronizing them) for this reality and the fact that your teen is unlikely to be as articulate as you are.
  - Remember that negotiations work best when both parties start in a calm mood – so do your deep breathing and choose the calmest moment and spot you can find.
  - It helps to know each other's needs before you start negotiating. Your child, however, may not be able to express these, so give some thought to their needs yourself.

- **When going for the deal:**
  - Adopt a non-threatening but 'business-like' body stance: if you look too laid back, your 'talk' will not be taken so seriously. So look at ease but sit fairly upright and use direct (but not staring) eye contact if you can get it.

- Start by expressing the hope (or expectation) that you are going to reach an agreement. You can say, for example, *'I'm sure that once we have talked this through calmly we will come up with some kind of solution together.'*

     If this is the tenth time you have tried to negotiate this particular issue, you may need to try another tack! Include the negative consequences that could result from not reaching a deal. For example, *'I do hope we find some way of resolving this today because, if we don't, the atmosphere between us is going to drag on and on. I certainly don't want to go through Christmas like this, and I'm sure you don't'* or *'If we don't work out something today, dad and I are just going to have to make a decision without you. It is too important to be left to drag on and on.'*

- State your needs in a very direct way. For example, *'I want to know that you are going to be safe and not too tired to concentrate on your work the next day.'*

     Don't be hurt if they haven't thought of these: teens are essentially egocentric. When others' needs are pointed out to them, they can be surprisingly accepting.

- Hazard a guess about their needs. Your aim is to start them thinking about this, so don't worry about guessing exactly right – trust that they'll tell you if you get it wrong! For example, *'I guess you don't want to feel you have missed out on something all your friends seem to be doing, is that right?'*

- Listen attentively (and use the skills outlined in Rule 3 to show them that you are). Don't forget to check out that you are reading between the lines correctly.

- State what you *ideally* want. Remember that you are going to have to give a little in order to reach a deal. So this should not be your 'bottom line' position.

- Listen again.

- Acknowledge their position and feelings: this is about showing empathy with them. You can say, for example, *'I can see that it's an awkward situation and you're hurt because you think I can't trust you.'*

- Try to find some common ground. For example, *'We both think you deserve some fun and should go to the party.'*
- Suggest a compromise – ask first for their idea. If they are not forthcoming (and often they are not) propose one yourself. For example, *'How about this time we make it 11.30 instead of midnight? – and I'll offer to take some of your friends home as well which will save you the taxi fares.'*

■ **When a deal has been struck:**
- Round off positively with a specific compliment – even if the deal was reached after much tortuous exchange and agreed very grudgingly. For example, *'It's great that we have agreed. I think you did really well to keep your cool'* or *'I'm so pleased that's behind us now – I admired the way you argued your case even if I can't still agree with you on everything.'*

■ **When the conflict is still unresolved:**
- Round off your negotiation as positively as you can: don't let it develop into an argument or stony silence. Make it clear that you are finishing this interaction (this is another communication skill that teenagers have to learn). This will make it easier for you to carry on living together while the conflict is still unresolved. For example, *'Well, I think we have really had a good honest talk about this and got as far as we can for the minute. Shall I make us a coffee and we can watch "Eastenders" now.'*
- Give them time to think; teenagers often prefer this to 'backing down' immediately. It also gives them time to calm down and think through the options very carefully. For example: *'I'd like you to just think about what I've suggested and let me know tomorrow morning if we've got a deal.'*
- Stick to your guns when you reach your bottom line; it is ultimately your responsibility as a parent to do this. For example, *'I think we have both tried our very best to sort this out together and I'm sorry we couldn't agree. We obviously both have such different views on the subject. But now we have to resolve the issue*

and as your parent, it is ultimately my responsibility to look after
you in the best way I know how. So I'm afraid I still want you to return
by 11 pm.'

'I actually think that some of the battles that we had brought us closer together – when I kept trying to assert myself and would not pretend to be anything but me, it must have been awful for you then, but I feel you really know me now.'

young adult writing to her mother

Rule 7:
Help Them to Discover their *Own* 'Carrots' and 'Sticks'

> I want you to know that if you see something worthwhile in what I am doing, it is not by accident but because of real direction and purpose.'
>
> Vincent Van Gogh

There is one personal story which always comes to mind when I think about this subject. A number of years ago when I brought out my first edition of *Confident Children*, my 16-year-old daughter, Laura, sometimes accompanied me on my publicity tours. As the book was dedicated to her and she was considering a career in the media, we both thought it would be a good opportunity for her to survey the scene first hand. Of course, quite understandably, journalists were keen to see how confident she was and what she had to say on the subject. I'll always remember her recounting this illustrative story to a TV interviewer – something I had never heard her talk about before.

Laura told the interviewer that the previous week she had been travelling home on the school bus and was listening to everyone's conversation as they nervously clutched the reports they had just been given:

> *'The main topic of conversation was about how their parents were going to react. Listening to them made me realize that I probably am a lot more self-confident than most people of my age. What was uppermost in my mind was whether my results would help me get onto the course which I wanted to do. I hadn't even thought about my parents' reaction.*
>
> *... Of course I like it when they're pleased, but that's not what makes me want to work hard or not ... it's my life, isn't it? I think wanting to do well for yourself and not just for your parents is one of the signs of confidence.'*

I felt a great weight lift off my shoulders when I heard this. I obviously felt very proud of her, but it was my own feeling of freedom which took me most by surprise. It made me realize how letting go of the responsibility of having to motivate our children is good for us as well as for them! For those of you who have not reached this point, I hope you will remember this because I know that passing on that responsibility is both a hard and a scary thing to do.

You may find that you have done or are doing much of the groundwork already. If not, here are some pointers which I hope will help.

Letting go of the responsibility of motivating our teens is good for us as well as for them!

Top Tips
- **Always focus on nurturing their best character traits** – rather than giving rewards and punishments for achieving or not achieving specific goals. (I have listed examples of the twelve most important character traits on pages 49–51.) In practise, this may mean boosting their self-esteem or suggesting better ways to organize their work rather than offering a 'bribe' of extra money or threatening them with a withdrawal of privileges.

In the long run, I assure you that this approach will pay off. In the short-term, it will take some willpower to put into practise. This is because 'carrots' and 'sticks' offered by parents often work well as quick-fixes – fear and greed will get any of us moving in the short-term – but this approach does not help our teens to develop willpower. It also fosters a dependence on those who have the power to entice and frighten them. And the downside for you is that you will eventually become resentful, tired and possibly broke!

You may also find it helpful to look at a copy of one of my earlier books, *Self Motivation*. It is a self-help programme designed to strengthen the 36 key characteristics and skills consistently displayed by self-motivated people. At an appropriate age, your teen might find a copy of the audio version useful.

- **Remember that what motivates you may not drive them** – although it could help to share your own 'tricks' if you make it clear that they will have to find their own.

- **Use their current heroes** – find out why they admire them. If they don't know much about them, you could help them do some research to see what has helped them become successful. It is rarely just luck or fashion that keeps successful people at the top. Self-motivation often plays a great part. The Internet is full of interviews and stories about how famous people 'made it'.

  You may of course also know some of the people they most admire (for example, a best friend or their soccer coach). You could suggest that they ask them for ideas about what to do when the going gets tough and encourage them to use this information when their own motivation is running low. For example:
  'What do you think ___ would do if he or she was feeling like this now?'
  'You said you admired ___ because he was always so organized. Do you think it would help if you ... ?'
  'Do you remember that in that article ___ said one of the secrets of his success was that he always tried to ... ?'

- **When they get it right, help them to reflect on why**. For example: *'You seemed to have no trouble in getting down to that essay. I wonder why it was easier for you to do your homework this week?'*

- **Remind them of things they have done in the past that helped**. For example: *'Do you remember that during the exams last term, you found that thinking about ... and not doing ... really seemed to help you?'*

- **Hold back on negative feedback** – until you have encouraged them first to reflect and make their own assessment. For example: *'Do you think it is helping you to get going by putting yourself down all the time?'* (instead of, *'You shouldn't put yourself down, it doesn't help'*) or,
'Do you think you have lost interest partly because you are so tired?' (instead of, *'If you got to bed earlier, you would feel differently'*).

- **Copy the following list of characteristics and suggestions** – and put it somewhere where you can see it regularly for a while. Discuss it with your partner and work out what you can do together to encourage your teen to be more self-motivated. If your teen is old enough you may want to share the list with them.

12 key characteristics of self-motivated people – and how you can help your teen to develop them

1. *Visionary Thinking*
   - encourage them to pursue realistic life-dreams and set long-term goals

2. *Optimism*
   - challenge their negative thinking, even when the going is tough

3. Sound Self-esteem
- confirm and remind them that they deserve success and have a right to be treated with respect

4. Thirst for Challenge
- extend their horizons and help them to set goals which stretch their potential

5. Consistent Courage
- refrain from being over-protective and show them how to manage the anxiety and fear of risk-taking. (See Rules 13 and 15)

6. Endless Energy
- encourage (but don't nag!) them to keep fit, well-fed and rested

7. Systematic Organization
- help them to establish reliable routines, procedures and methods

8. Meticulous Planning
- show them how to prepare outlines, strategies and step-by-step action plans

9. Sharp Decisiveness
- demonstrate how to use decision-making techniques and make contingency plans. (See Rule 8)

10. Searching Self-reflection
- encourage them to read their own minds and resist the temptation to explain their behaviour/beliefs and emotional responses to them

11. Sincere Self-forgiveness
- challenge self-punitive behaviour and encourage them to learn from their mistakes and move on

12. Revelling in Success

– encourage them not to hide their light under a bushel and help them to celebrate every success, however small. (See Rule 19)

'I found saying things like, "You can do it because I know you really want to pass, don't you?" much more motivating than the threats I used, such as, "If you don't get down to it, you'll fail."'

parent who had been on a parenting course

Rule 8:
Use 'Pull' not 'Push' to Help Them
with Difficult Choices

Making decisions and resolving dilemmas are central concerns for teenagers. Perhaps for the first time in their lives they are expected to take responsibility for making complex choices, which both they and we know may affect the rest of their lives. These could include:

- choosing between several tempting and feasible career paths
- choosing between two people they love such as friends, lovers or even parents
- deciding whether to take drugs or not
- deciding whether to become fully sexually active or not
- choosing whether to live or die (flirtation with this choice is common at this age, but with the increasing rates of depression and suicide it is now something which must be taken much more seriously).

When we see our deeply loved children facing such momentous choices, it is hard to sit back and let them 'do their own thing'. It is highly tempting to seize whatever power we think we have to try to push them in the direction we believe is right. In panic, many hither-to liberal parents may find themselves now banning contact with certain people, insisting that they take a particular course, or rifling through their child's bedroom in search of 'evidence'. They may do this in spite of the fact that they already know from bitter experience that this kind of action can:

- make a teen want to do the very opposite of what we want them to do. They feel disempowered and angry
- stop our children confiding in us about their serious dilemmas. This may mean that they will (or they may feel they) have no one to support them, should they make the wrong choice.

But don't forget that 'doing nothing' is not the only available alternative (even though it often feels that way). You can still do a great deal to help by channelling your concern and love into a 'pull' style of action. Here are some tips to show you how.

Top Tips

■ **Give their self-esteem a boost** – people with high self-esteem are more likely to choose options which are self-nurturing and not self-destructive. Here are some easy ways you can give your teen's self-esteem a boost.

---

10 quick ways to give your teen's self-esteem a boost

1. Stop what you are doing and listen and listen.
2. Give them an example of *why* you love, like and admire them.
3. Remind them of one of their strengths which they themselves have acknowledged.
4. Recall one or two of their hard-won past achievements.
5. Remind them of good feedback they received from someone else, such as a teacher or one of their friends.
6. Let them overhear you speaking warmly about them to someone else.
7. Make them their favourite meal.
8. Ask for their advice or opinion.
9. Buy and wrap them a mini-present for no reason at all.
10. Write them an encouraging card and leave it some place unexpected for them to find.

■ **Share your anxiety** – but avoid using overtones of emotional blackmail. If they love you, trust that upsetting or worrying you is not something they will want to readily do. For example:
'I can't deny that I am anxious about you doing ___ but that's my problem. I know that it is your decision and your life. I will be behind you whatever ...' (rather than, *'I've already had three sleepless nights over this; I don't think I could bear it if you ...'*).

- **Remind them of their key values** – without the sermon of course!

- **Give them inspirational examples** – tell them anecdotes about people you know of who have struggled successfully with similar issues. Buy or borrow suitable autobiographies (for example, a revered pop star's story of their dilemma on the drug issue or a famous person who played too safe or too riskily with their career path). Alternatively, arrange for them to meet a responsible, sensitive adult you know who has been through a similar experience (for example, a relative or friend whose life was affected by the birth of an unwanted baby or a colleague who gave up a certain course at school/college. But whatever you do, be clear with the person that the purpose of the talk with your teen is to give them information and insight and not to tell them which way they must choose.

> 'It is your job to help your teenager make their *own* decisions, not to make their decisions for them ... engage them in conversation and present your advice in the form of relaxed questions and suggestions.'
>
> Steve Chalke

- **Encourage them to rest and relax** – explain that being in a state of anxiety will inhibit their ability to think clearly. All serious decision-making puts a strain on our bodies, so they may need extra care and nurturing through this period.

- **Demonstrate decision-making techniques** – you probably have developed your own favourite by now. Tell them about how it has helped you. If you want another example, here is a strategy which you could copy and give to them. But I suggest that, before doing so, you experiment with using it yourself!

A decision-making strategy

1. Find several sheets of paper, pencils and a rubber (unless you are so computer literate that you would prefer to do this exercise on screen).
2. Brainstorm all the different issues involved in the decision. This means randomly jotting down on paper any word that comes to mind without analysing why or making a value judgement about it. The issues could be very wide-ranging (for example, health, money, self-esteem, hurting others, loyalty, fears, and so forth).
3. Divide another piece of paper into four columns.
4. In the first column list the issues, leaving aside the ones which you may no longer consider relevant.
5. In the second column enter a grading (perhaps 1-10 score), which would reflect the issue's importance in terms of your *current* needs and concerns.
6. In the third column give them another grade in terms of their feel-good factor. This will help you ascertain whether your heart is playing a more or less significant role than your head in making this important decision.
7. In the fourth column enter a grading which is relevant to your long-term goals and your life-dream.
8. Then take another piece of paper and divide into four columns again. This time list your options and then complete steps 5-7 for each of these.
9. Compare your grades and make your decision.
10. Make a contingency plan. Work out what positive action you could take to help you survive if it turns out you have made the wrong decision or fate intervenes with a negative twist to thwart your plans.

- **Buy or lend them a book on the subject** – there is a good one listed in my *Recommended Reading* section at the end of the book.

- **Find some support for yourself** – talk through your own anxiety about their dilemma with a friend or your partner, or even someone like their teacher. This may help you to restrain your understandable urge to 'push' them in the direction which *you* think is right.

'People are usually more convinced by reasons they discover them-selves than by those found by others.'

Blaise Pascal

Rule 9:
Ask for Their Help on *Their* Terms

> 'One way to detect and boost kids' natural abilities is by offering them meaningful work within the family ... when they complain about doing chores, parents would do well to consider what kind of work they are asking their young teens to do.'
>
> Laura Sessions Stepp, *Our Last Best Shot*

You must yourself have felt many, many times that great swell of pride and self-satisfaction that comes from helping people you have never met. Every time I receive a letter of appreciation from an unknown person, I feel as though I have grown a foot taller! But don't these feelings pale into insignificance beside the boost we get when we find an opportunity to help someone we love who has helped *us* when we needed them to do so?

You can probably also recall the days when it was so easy to give your child the opportunity to feel this kind of boost to their self-esteem. I'm sure you can recall with nostalgia their proud face when they cleared the table or brought you a cup of tea in bed for the first time on your birthday. In contrast, nowadays all you may be aware of is how little your teenager seems to want to do to help you!

It's hard to believe sometimes that beneath all that egocentric thinking and the rebellion about household chores, there still lurks the 'heart of gold'. But it is worth reinforcing this belief because it will help motivate you to keep on trying. You can do so much more than just sit and wait for their 'selfish phase' to pass. Firstly, you can try to improve or adapt the way you ask for help and secondly, you can try to think more creatively and pragmatically about the ways in which you might be able to use their help. I hope these tips will help you to do both. I can give no guarantees, but trust that they are ones that have worked for other parents who were tired to death of endless battles about uncut lawns and mucky bathrooms.

Top Tips

- **Make sure that your need is a genuine one** – if you are asking them just for the sake of building their confidence, they may feel patronized and therefore belittled. It will not be an uplifting experience for either party.

- **Be realistic – don't wait for a philanthropic miracle!** Accept that teens are egocentric in their thinking and their behaviour. They usually need to be *asked* for help and they may need to be given feedback when they are depriving you of it. (For example, *'I'd like you to help with the shopping this week. It's three weeks since we have gone to the supermarket together and I find it so much more tiring doing it by myself.'*) During these years they are less likely to spontaneously volunteer their help than at any other time of their life. Remind yourself that this does not mean that their personality has radically transformed itself overnight into that of a selfish and insensitive creature. Helping others may not be top of their priority list at the moment, but that does not mean that they are incapable of feeling proud when they do help and guilty when they don't (even though they may do their utmost to hide such feelings from you and the world).

- **Accept that *for the time being*, you may not get the type of help you need *most*** – however assertively you may ask for it. You may have to settle for getting a different kind of help – the kind that is easier for them to currently give, for example, asking for their advice about a family issue or asking them to teach you a new skill (see tips below). So this may mean putting aside your resentment about their unwillingness to take their fair share of the more boring and tedious chores, which would take the most pressure off you. Once they have 'reconnected' with the part of them that does enjoy helping, you may find that they are generally more willing to help in other areas.

- **Ask them to teach you something** – this is an excellent way to give their self-esteem a boost. Maybe you could ask them about an aspect of their academic work (this should not be hard to find if you look at their curriculum). There is bound to be some area of their new knowledge which could be of interest or help to you, for example, some fascinating new research about the workings of our mind or body. Alternatively, they could coach you in one of their skills, for example, computer literacy, goal scoring or playing an instrument.

Ask their advice on current fashion trends – you could (within reason!) use their help to update your wardrobe or your house décor. I used my daughter to help me choose more up-to-date covers and colours for my books and tapes. Her choices proved to be excellent.

- **Consult them about your own dilemmas at work** – their fresh approach can be very enlightening, not to mention confronting. Perhaps their very lack of experience helps them to see through to the heart of the matter more easily. One of my daughters had a very logical and analytical mind and as a young teen would tell me straight whenever my emotions had warped my thinking and were masking the reality of certain situations. The other had a great gut instinct for sounding out genuineness. She was extremely useful in alerting me to people who were 'pulling a fast one' (I have a tendency to trust much too easily).

- **Ask them to help you talk through extended family problems and worries** – teenagers can be particularly helpful, in my experience, with relationships with their grandparents' generation. The bigger generation gap seems to enable them to often be more empathic and sensitive to their issues and needs. But also their acute sense of justice can be very supportive when they feel *you* are being unjustly blamed or having your guilt buttons pressed.

- **Before making a request for help, check your body language** – make sure that it is transmitting a confident, positive message. (This is important if you are asking for help with

something that you know they are not going to want to do!) This means no whiny tones or pathetic appealing eyes or threatening gestures, however depressed or provoked you might feel. Think yourself into an optimistic mood by imagining the best possible outcome. This will help you to stand naturally tall and look relaxed. Stretch your imagination and visualize receiving a cheerful response and an agreement to do whatever you ask – immediately! Seriously, we know that matching an assertive request with positive non-verbal communication can increase our chances of being successful.

- **Don't beat about the bush** – briskly summarize your problem or need in one sentence, or two at the most. For example: *'I have to work on Tuesday evening this week. I won't be able to take Julie to her music lesson.'* Leave out the preliminary long lecture or reminder of previous disappointments. For instance: *'Families should pull together. We work very hard to see that you ...' / 'I've been* *asking you for weeks if you could help me with ferrying Julie to her lessons, but you always say you are too busy, but I'll ask you again ...'.* However well-deserved, these are a big 'switch-off'.

- **Show appreciation of their feelings or problems** – don't assume that because you love them, they know you have thought about their side of the situation sympathetically. Put your empathy into words. For example: *'I can see that you are busy ...'* / *'I know you hate doing ...'.*

- **Use simple, straightforward and direct language** – and use the first person so it is clear that it is something *you* want or need. Avoid hints, patronizing flattery, or implying a 'should' or 'ought'. For example: *'I'd like you to help me with the shopping on Saturday before you go off to ...'.* (Instead of: *'Oh dear, there's all the shopping to do on Saturday as well as everything else. I'll be exhausted'/ 'It would be so nice if you could help me with the shopping, you're so good at it.' / 'Jim Taylor always drives his mum to the hypermarket on Saturdays').*

- **Round off your requests on a positive note** – point out what the pay-off for them might be if they do what you have asked. This may simply be that you will be pleased and the nagging will stop. Or, it could be more directly rewarding, for example: *'You could get that new CD while you are there – they are cheaper there than in town.'*

Rule 10:
Prove Your Commitment with
Time that You Think You Can't Spare

A number of years ago I made a simple life rule for myself, which has proved to be one of the greatest guiding forces I have ever had in my life. It was:

'To spend more time than I think I can afford on the relationships which matter most to me.'

I made it at a time when my second daughter was halfway through her teens. I wish I had made it earlier – it would have saved me so much angst and guilt. I also know it would have helped me to set aside even more of my time to spend with my daughters. Although it may sound trite and obvious to say it, there is no better way to show your love and support than by giving what today is often our most precious resource – time. This is especially true if you are a busy person with an active and full life of your own.

Of course, I am not advocating that you should routinely martyr yourself to your teenager's *every* demand for your attention and presence. That would be bad for them as well as you. But always remember the power you have to build their self-esteem by just giving them gifts of time. It is an important way of demonstrating (rather than just telling them) that they are, and will always be, at the top end of your priorities.

There is no better way to show your love and support for your teen than by spending time with them.

There are several reasons why even the most dedicated parents often need to be reminded of this power when their children are teenagers.

Firstly, they may not appear to appreciate our presence in the way that they did before. One of our family's rituals was that, in spite of being a working mum, the girls and I would have afternoon tea together when they returned home from school. This used to be a wonderfully rewarding experience when they were younger. We cuddled up on the sofa and listened to each others stories about the day. However, when they reached their teenage years, I found it much harder to 'justify' the time. The experience was so different. We would sit mostly in silence. They would often appear glued to daytime TV programmes which I considered to be fatuous and mind-numbing. The only sounds from them appeared to come in the form of long moans about their friends, teachers and their 'BORING' schoolwork. My interventions often seemed to increase rather than relieve their irritation.

Inevitably, my mind would start to dwell on all the many other tasks I could be finishing in my office downstairs or in the kitchen. I had to force myself to stay sitting on the sofa. It was hard to trust my instinct, which told me that being present for the girls at this time of day was vitally important even though it might not appear to be so.

Thank goodness I did stick it out. In their later years, they have expressed plenty of appreciation for these kinds of times. They have told me that these after-school times together provided a very stabilizing anchor for them amidst the angst and chaos of their lives. Of course, I wish they could have said this at the time. But they couldn't. In spite of their mature appearance and manner, not only did they lack the vocabulary to express such appreciation, they had no real awareness of their need and no way of assessing the value of the time I was giving.

Secondly, this is a time when often we are at our busiest and we know our children can now survive without us. If we have a career, it will usually mean that our job now carries much more responsibility. If we haven't, by now we are probably locked into dozens of other voluntary commitments.

Every busy loving parent will find time for their children when their dependency and needs are highly apparent. But, if we are honest, isn't it much more tempting to find something more pressing to do than spend time with a teen who is perfectly competent to look after themselves, has a social diary we ourselves would die for, and still finds the time to stare for hours on end at just one zit?!

Thirdly, it is a time which often coincides with our own mid-life crises. It is at this time that we begin to become more aware of the tick of the biological clock and our own impermanence! Perhaps our parents and some of our friends have already died. Our hair is probably distinctly grey and we have to work that much harder to keep fit and remember what we were supposed to do today. Commonly, we start to reflect on our regrets and lost opportunities. Watching our teenagers making their future plans can rub salt into these festering wounds. They remind us of all the hopes we once had at their age which may have become sidelined throughout our parenting and mortgage-paying years.

If your own adolescence was different, perhaps more restricted and less hopeful, the urge to make up for lost time may be even greater. And as our needs affect our perception, you may be less likely to notice how much your teenager still needs your presence. I hope in making this point I haven't been pushing too many guilt buttons. But, as a therapist, I have seen too many genuinely caring parents with this problem to leave it aside.

The trick, as always, is to find the right balance. Each of us has to use our individual consciences together with our diaries and budgets to find this balance. Even then we will get it wrong sometimes. It is not easy. It takes time and much experimenting to find it. But I hope that having this rule uppermost in your mind will help you to achieve this as much as it has helped me.

Top Tips

- **Make yourself a snappy time 'rule'** – this doesn't have to be the same as my rule, which I shared with you earlier. Compose one that will work for you because it is relevant to your life and will remind you of your priorities. Say it to yourself frequently over the next month to fix it firmly in your mind. In addition, write it down somewhere where you will see it regularly, as this will help fix it in your subconscious mind as well. If possible 'go public' with it, so your friends and family and even your teenager can help you to keep to it.

■ **Agree some 'sacred' times when you will be available for a chat** – even if this is only sharing a cup of coffee together. One set of parents in my survey made this last-drink-of-the-night time and, (unlike me!), stayed up dutifully until each teen was home. Your teen may not always welcome your company or want to talk then, but at least they will know that it is their time and it is available if they need it. One of our times was Sunday breakfast, but this had to become a moveable feast as Saturday nights became later and later. If you can't be around at your special time, sincerely apologizing for not being there is a very good second-best self-esteem boost.

■ **Make opportunities for special one-to-one social time** – I know this is difficult if you have a big family, but of course it is even more important then to do so. Younger children often want to be glued to their older brother or sister and will try to tag on to this one-to-one time. Resist if you can, even if your teenager gives in to their pleas. Giving them this special 'adult' time with you is a way of showing respect for their new mature status. And you will both need these times alone together if you want to preserve the closeness of your relationship during these transitional years. If both parents are in the picture, each should have their own one-to-one time, but it is especially important for role-modelling reasons that sons have extra time with their fathers, and daughters with their mothers.

■ **Lower some standards to create the extra time you will need** – this is a reminder tip for perfectionists! As a self-confessed member of this neurotic set, I know it is necessary. Be assured there will be plenty of time to 'Go for Gold' when your children have left home. In the meantime, look at some areas in your life where bronze standards could be good enough. An obvious one might be house maintenance and cleaning, but others could be training courses or hobbies and certain work projects.

- **Delegate and delegate some more** – in order to create even more time to be with your teen. I know this may sound an obvious one, but I have seen too many unnecessarily over-stretched parents not to include it. Many people are reluctant to ask their family and friends for help unless they are desperate, even though they suspect that they would willingly give an extra hand. Others won't employ cleaners or gardeners or sitters for the younger children, not because they can't afford to do so, but because they don't like to trust others to do their work. Push through these internal barriers because time with your teen should be a high priority, however frivolous the activity you do together may seem.

> 'We found that when his self-esteem was low, just making time to do things together that we know he enjoyed, such as playing a board game, really helped. I suppose it showed him that he was loved and important.'
>
> mother of teen

Rule 11:
Be Content to be a Predictable Parent
rather than a Best Mate

'I've suddenly realized what is wrong with her. Mother has said she sees us more as friends than as daughters. That's all very nice of course, except that a friend can't take the place of a mother. I need my mother to be a good example and someone I can respect.'

Anne Frank

We have already spent much of this book focusing on the difficulties we often encounter when parenting a teen. This is not surprising considering I am writing, and you are reading, a problem-solving book! But, as I hope most of you know by now, life with children of this age can also be fantastic fun and very exhilarating. In spite of all the stresses and worry, these years undoubtedly rejuvenated me as they commonly do many other parents. I found my daughters and their friends more exciting and stimulating to be with at this age than at any other. Our lengthy and lively debates were often deeply challenging and I found myself reviewing many stale ideas and dated values. Their zest for life and their idealism was infectious, and it was no coincidence that it was during these years that I started several exciting new projects.

I also felt rejuvenated as a woman as their influence and encouragement steered me towards more flattering and trendy clothes and make-up. I felt flattered when I was included as 'one of the gang' when we sat around having coffee together. But I felt even more privileged and enthralled when they chose to talk on a deeply intimate level with me about their relationships and their inner fears and concerns.

In short, I often felt like a teenager myself again. The friendship I was developing with my daughters was both cocooning and liberating. In many ways it felt very similar to the deeply intimate relationships I had had with my closest friends when I was their age. Fortunately, partly because of the trade I am in, warning bells started to ring in time.

For many years, I had been witness to many of the pitfalls that can arise by allowing such relationships to drift into 'best mate' status. I had heard parents expressing their guilt and regret because, with hindsight, they could see that their overly close relationships had blinded them from protecting their children against their wilder selves. I had seen teens themselves become mistrustful and angry with parents, because they felt they were two-faced. One minute they were their 'best pals' and the next they were laying the law down in an authoritarian manner. I had heard others wishing their parents had been 'more grown-up like other parents' and even complaining that they would rather they had been stricter.

But perhaps more commonly, I have seen how being too closely bonded to a parent can have a restricting effect on the development of the teen's adult personality. We have already noted that one of the ways we become 'our own person' is by exploring the differences between our parents and ourselves. This inevitably involves challenging their values, beliefs and rules, as well as spending longer and longer periods away from them. All this is obviously much harder to do if your relationship has the interdependency that being best mates implies.

Top Tips

- **Accept that your teen needs, at least sometimes, to *perceive* you as predictable (or, as they may well put it, 'BORING!')** This is a trait that is rarely attributed to best mates! In their rapidly changing inner and outer world, it is wonderfully reassuring for them to believe that they can rely on mum and/or dad to be essentially the same as they were yesterday and to most likely be the same tomorrow.

  Of course, in order to be able to withstand the put-downs and perhaps unfair assessment of our dynamic personalities by our teens, we need to make sure that our own confidence is constantly boosted. This is yet another good reason for giving Rule 1 high priority. It helps us to judge ourselves for who we *know* we are rather than the kind of stick-in-the-mud our teen currently needs to think we are!

'You may think that they treat you like a fossil – they may even think of you as a fossil – but actually you are a rock ... in the midst of this sea of turmoil and confusion, it's your job as a parent to act as an anchor.'

Steve Chalke

- **Think carefully before deciding to be on first name terms**. It is understandable for teenagers to want to change the way they refer to you. They are looking for symbols which indicate that they have moved from child into adult status. The transition state they are in can feel very uncomfortable and insecure. It is also understandable for parents to want to do a little re-labelling for the same reason. But, of course, the reality is that although many aspects of the relationship have changed, the essential elements don't, and through these transitional years children need to have confidence that these elements are still there. Calling parents by a special name psychologically reinforces the fact that:
  - parents are still in charge and responsible for their care. (This is until they reach the age of 16 – though children do not reach full adult status until two years later, and even then, most still remain very dependent for many years after that.)
  - their parents belong to them and that they always have done and always will. The use of *my* mum and *my* dad and even *my* step-mum and *my* step-dad suggests a unique sense of belonging.

  Instead of moving on to first names terms, you could try a variation. A common one in my country is to move on from mummy and daddy to mother and father during this period. Other people find they develop special nicknames or indeed do the opposite and abandon the ones developed for each other in childhood.

- **Ensure that you both have plenty of other friends**. Of course, the more satisfying your own friendship network is, the less you will *need* your teen to be your mate rather than your child. So make sure that no matter how busy and stressed you may be that you spend time with your friends as well.

If your teen lacks confidence, he or she may be holding back from developing a friendship, and it is your job to encourage them to do so. One or two friends should be fulfilling a more intimate 'best mate' role. When your teen shares something special with you, suggest that they could also tell their friend, ___ , about it. You could also suggest activities that they could do together which you have always previously done with them. For example, you could make it easy for them by offering to drop them off at the shopping centre or football match. Then (assuming their outing went well) when you pick them up you can talk about what a great time you had when you went out recently with your best friend!

You could also talk about the friends you had when you were their age and why they were special. If you didn't have that experience you can talk about how much it would have meant to you to have had a special friend of your own age at that time.

Under-confident children often need quite a few of these gentle 'pushes' from their parents before they find a best friend they can trust. There are the obvious reasons why this should be so, such as their lack of self-esteem or their lower level of social skills. But it could also be because they have had a very close relationship with their mother or father throughout their childhood and have less need of friends.

Children who have been through a major trauma such as a divorce or bereavement may also need more encouragement because they have lost some of their trust in relationships.

Rule 12:
Stay Honest and Focused When
Giving Feedback

'Young people who are in the process of developing explanations of their success and failures are particularly vulnerable to what is being told to them about themselves. They are dependent on good feedback to construct a respectful view of themselves.'

Jacki Gordon and Gillian Grant, *How We Feel*

You will remember from the *What Exactly is Confidence?* chapter that sound self-knowledge is an important component of inner confidence. You can help your teen a great deal in this area by giving them good quality feedback. This is such an important time for them in terms of establishing their own sense of identity and developing an accurate and realistic view of their strengths and weaknesses.

Teens need feedback to help them develop a realistic view of their strengths and weaknesses.

But giving feedback to a teen can be hard work and sometimes very unrewarding. They often appear not to want to know or care about what you have to say. Even our well-meant compliments have a habit of bouncing irritably back in our faces.

'I'm not pretty – can't you see these spots?'

'It's not good ... it's crap ... and anyway what do you know about it? The curriculum has changed a little since the dark ages, you know.'

One hurtful quip from my daughter that I remember very well was:

'Well, you're my mother, aren't you? You have to think that.'

I later discovered that this was a retort that is commonly received by well-meaning parents all over the world!

Giving criticism can be even more difficult. Even in its mildest form it often sparks off scornful laughter, retaliatory abuse, tantrums or, alternatively, prolonged sulks or incapacitating depression. So is it surprising that so many parents stop trying? It is understandable that so many end up saying, *'I'm just going to keep my mouth shut – it's not worth the hassle.'*

But, of course, it is worth the hassle. Teens desperately need feedback and they also need to learn how to give and receive it. However unrewarding the task is in the short-term, it is worth persisting. I hope my tips will help make this just a little bit easier to do. If you find that your words are repeatedly falling on stony or angry ground, you can use them to check that you are giving your feedback in a way that is most likely to be effective.

Don't forget that giving good feedback is something that even the most senior and successful captains of industry are still very bad at. I know because I have been giving them courses in this art for many years. So, if you do get it wrong from time to time, or even frequently, remember it is always possible to rectify the situation and use it as a learning opportunity. A simple apology and a rephrased compliment or criticism is a brilliant way of demonstrating the difference between good and bad feedback.

Top Tips

On giving compliments

- **Choose your moment carefully** – giving a compliment as soon as it pops into your head may not be the ideal time for it to be received. You may not be in the right kind of company or your teen may be too busy, preoccupied, anxious, depressed or even excited to able to take it in.

  If it is an important one, store it up and give it when you find a quiet reflective moment (well, relatively quiet!). Alternatively, use a time when you are both comfortably engaged in an activity together such as driving somewhere, walking to town or clearing the kitchen.

Don't forget that you don't always have to respond immediately to a request for feedback from your teen, even for the positive kind. You may be able to use feedback to build their confidence in a more meaningful way if you take time to reflect and compose what you want to say. For example, if they ask you what you think of an essay, say on first glance it looks great, but you'd like some time to look at it properly. Your feedback could then be focused around an aspect of them which you may know needs strengthening, such as their sticking power or ability to organize themselves.

- **Take it easy** – teens who lack confidence often feel excruciatingly embarrassed on hearing a compliment. (That's the emotional fuel driving not just the blushes, but also the smart retaliatory quips.) One of the ways you can lessen their pain a little is by looking and sounding extremely at ease in the situation yourself. Adopt a more take-it-or-leave-it and matter of fact tone than perhaps you would use when giving a compliment to a more confident adult. Don't expect eye contact or a straight assertive 'thank-you'. (You can always show your teen how to accept compliments through role-modelling.) Routinely drop appreciative comments casually into conversations.

- **Spell out the 'whys' and the 'wherefores'** – try and be as specific as you can when giving positive feedback. For example, *'I love you'* has more impact if it is followed by an 'explanation', such as: *'... you're so much fun to be with'* or *'... you continually amaze me with your courage.'*

  Similarly, *'Well done – that's an excellent report. I'm proud of you'* has more meaning if you add a remark, such as: *'I am particularly pleased with the comments about how hard you tried in maths and your improved grade in biology. I know both of these are difficult subjects for you.'*

- **Write them down** – seize and make opportunities to put your appreciations on paper. This may seem a strange thing to do with people we have face-to-face contact with every day. It is also becoming an increasingly unusual thing to do even when we are away. But written compliments and appreciations can have a huge impact on people with low self-esteem. They can be looked at again and again. We also know that any information is likely to be firmly recorded in our brain's memory if it is received by more than one of our senses. Try one or two (if not all!) of these ideas:

– adding compliments to birthday and Christmas cards
– keeping a store of blank cards and post-it notes handy and jotting down appreciations for them to find when you are not there
– adding compliments to reminder notes (For example: *'Don't forget your dental appt at 2 pm – by the way you looked great this morning in that new shirt.'*)
– giving thank-you cards and notes attached perhaps to a small treat when they have done something especially kind or helpful (For example: *'Thanks again for dropping my cleaning off – I really appreciated the help, I was in such a panic to get the train – enjoy the cake!'*)
– sending postcards with appreciations when you or they go away, even though you may talk to them on the phone every day
– using text messages to leave appreciations on their mobile phone

■ **Don't include a put-down of you or anyone else** – this is such common practise that you might find this a hard habit to crack. Ask your partner or even your teen themselves to tell you when you are doing it otherwise you won't probably notice you have added well-meaning tailpieces to your compliments. For example: *'I'm dreadful at that'* / *'No one else in this family seems to care'* / *'You stood out in the crowd – everyone else in your group looked scruffy'* / *'I don't think Jane could have done that, she's too ...'*. At their best, such add-on remarks distract from the main message of your positive feedback and at their worst, they can build arrogance instead of inner confidence!

- **Don't round off your compliment with a 'dig'** – this is so tempting to do, especially if we have been having a particular frustrating or trying time with our teen. Make sure you avoid tagging on a sting in the tail, such as: *'I only wish it was like that all the time' / 'If only you had done it earlier' / 'Now can we expect to see that again tomorrow or will we have to wait another year?'*

On giving constructive criticism

- **Start with a positive comment** – but be careful to be genuine. If you are still angry or upset it might be difficult to think of something, so wait until you have calmed down and perhaps talked through the problem with someone who can be a bit more detached. For example: *'You know I think you have been really trying hard recently ...' / 'You are generally a very kind person, but occasionally you ...'.*

- **Focus on behaviour that can be changed** – rather than general personality characteristics. You can say, for example: *'I get the impression that you don't think about how you might hurt people before you speak.'* (Instead of: *'You're so insensitive'*) *'I get really annoyed when you leave your shoes in the hall and your coat is thrown down on the chair in the sitting room. Could you take them upstairs to your room as soon as you get in?'* (Instead of: *'Why are you so untidy?'*)

- **Avoid exaggerations** – these are not only unfair, they are inflammatory and counter-productive. Using phrases like *'You always ...'* and *'You never ...'* are rarely justified and will immediately make your teen want to leap to his or her defence or pick holes in your 'case'.

- **Focus on a few specific recent examples** – when we start to give criticism, the temptation is to bring up all our grievances at the same time. The 'while I'm at it' game is one that cries out for two players, so by starting it you are inviting a slanging match. Instead, be content with giving just one or at the most two examples of the behaviour that you would like to see changed. For example: *'You were late setting off for school three times this week'* / *'You've interrupted me twice now – I keep losing my train of thought'*.

■ **Confront your teen with consequences and choices** – rather than giving lectures and dictates. You can say, for example: *'If you continue to be late as often as that, Mr Jones is going to call you in again for detention and you'll miss swimming.'* (Instead of: *'Don't be late this week like you were last week.'*)
'You haven't put your dirty washing in the linen basket again this week. I have said I am not going to hunt around in your room for it anymore. You can continue to leave it on the floor, but this means you will have no clean shirt for school on Monday. It's your choice.' (Instead of: *'I've told you week after week not to leave you dirty washing on your floor. I suppose this means we are going to have another Monday morning tantrum.'*)

■ **Use first person language whenever you can** – it is important to show that you take responsibility yourself for the feedback and do not pass the buck directly or indirectly to anyone else. For example, you can replace *'If the school head sees you behaving like this ...'* with an 'I' statement such as, *'I don't like to see you behaving in a way which ...'*. Or you can replace *'In my day, children of your age never ...'* with *'I wish you would ...'*.

■ **Rarely compare them to others** – even when they seduce you to do so. Teens are constantly looking over their shoulder. They look because they need to identify with a group outside their family. They look because they need to be accepted by their peers. And, of course, they often look because their inner confidence is shaky.

In our role as parents we can help them by countering these constant comparisons with the outside world by giving them feedback which doesn't use comparisons with others for benchmarking. The comparing we can encourage them to do and value is with their own past behaviour and performance. That is

not to say that they do not need to be aware of how they are doing in relation to the rest of the world. Of course they do. But they usually obtain plenty of this kind of evaluation during this period of their lives from others as well as themselves. Unless we believe these comparisons are grossly off the mark, or unjust, our energy is usually better diverted elsewhere. For example:

Teen: '... *Sam's been selected for the team – why can he manage it and I can't? He's so ... I'll never be able to ...*'

You: '*Well, let's not forget what you have achieved this year – you did ... and ... But maybe if you had attended as many training sessions as you did last year, you might have made it. What do you think?*'

> 'One thing that parents don't always seem to understand is how much it hurts to be compared to our brothers and sisters, and other relatives – to anyone, in fact, even simple comparisons can be painful.'
>
> Cassandra Walker Simmons, *Becoming Myself*

■ **Focus more attention on the inner rather than the outer them** – again, this is a matter of countering one of their common tendencies. Teenage 'obsession' with their outer appearance is such that sometimes we despair that they will ever again put any value on any other of their personal attributes or qualities. We worry that they have become shallow and superficial and only ever capable of judging themselves or others by their outer image. Giving them critical feedback in this area is perhaps the most unrewarding parenting task we can engage in. They may invite it all the time with questions such as *'Don't I look a mess?'* / *'Doesn't this make me look fat?'* / *'These spots are gross aren't they?'* – but (at best!) they ignore your reply.

So don't waste too much of your energy in this area. Instead, give them feedback centred around their mental, emotional and spiritual selves. You can be of more help by confronting them when you see them, for example, underachieving, thinking negatively or selling out on their values or hopes and dreams. Even though they may not readily show it, they are much more likely to listen to what you have to say in these areas than on the subject of their appearance.

Rule 13:
Be a Safety Net not a Security Blanket

'Good timber does not grow with ease; the stronger the wind, the stronger the trees.'

J. Willard Marriott

Journalists often ask me what is the biggest mistake parents tend to make. I usually hate these kinds of media questions which force me to generalize – but not this one. The answer comes easily and willingly. I am both convinced and concerned that nowadays the vast majority of the mistakes that I see being made by parents can be summarized in one word – **over-protection**.

Of course it is easy to see why this should be so. The world is becoming a much more frightening place to launch our children into. However much we may try to blame media hype for fanning our fears, we all know that there are some very real dangers confronting young people of today. For example:

- globalization and constant technological change have increased competitiveness and job insecurity so that aggression and bullying are not just playground phenomena but common in the workplace too
- the spread of addictive drugs has meant that pushers and violence on the streets are more prevalent
- our roads are so frustratingly congested that young people will take even more risks to get their thrills from speeding
- world travel is now so financially accessible that young people can wander into hazardous territory before they have the skills and know-how to defend themselves
- sexual liberation has helped to increase the possibility of abuse and life-threatening disease
- marketing and advertising has become so sophisticated that young minds are much more easily influenced to make decisions which may be counter to their own financial security and even their health.

But this is *their* brave new world. It is the world they will both *need* and *want* to enter. We must not frighten them sick about joining it. Neither must we hide its stark realities from them. It is our job, instead, to give them the best information, tools and resources to survive and thrive in it. We must let them take risks and give them the opportunity to learn from their mistakes.

These are truths that most parents know and accept in theory. But in their everyday practise, they often behave as though they believe they have the power to stop their children from coming face to face with these kinds of dangers. I did it myself. I rationed television; I forbade smoking and drug taking; I heard myself making put-downs of 'unsuitable friends' and talking more about the dangers of sex than its thrills. I tried to bribe one daughter away from backpacking holidays with an offer of prepaid hotels and I bought my other daughter the most boringly safe car to drive. Occasionally, I have to admit, I resorted as well to the kind of emotional blackmail I always believed I would never use. (*'I won't be able to sleep ...' / ' I don't think I could cope if you ...'*)

Fortunately, I had bred very assertive children who confronted me fairly and squarely. Firstly, they would face me with the limits of my power to enforce such sanctions and secondly, they argued forcibly in support of their rights. I was also lucky enough to have a very supportive partner. Together we worked out ways of controlling our fears rather than trying to control the uncontrollable dangers that our daughters were facing.

Work out ways to control *your* fears rather than trying to control the uncontrollable dangers that your teen faces.

But that was not the end of the story. The battle between our overprotective emotional urges and our rational decision-making capacities continued to erupt from time to time. The best we achieved was that we learned to recognize our over-protectiveness for what it was and we became more skilled at stopping it escalating out of control.

But however successful our efforts to build confidence in our children and control our own over-protective responses were, in the end they could not stop our own personal tragedy from occurring. We lost our daughter, Laura, like many parents before and after us have done. She was killed in the 'boring' car at the age of 19. She wasn't speeding down a motorway and she wasn't drunk or on drugs. She was driving down a country road a few miles from home. What happened to us can happen to any family. This is the stark truth that every parent and every teen has to find their way of living with.

So, the following tips can in no way guarantee that your teen will be safe or that your fear will disappear altogether. I hope, however, they might give you some ideas which will help you to manage your anxiety without smothering your teenager's adventurous spirit.

Top Tips

- **Remind yourself of the advantages of risk-taking** – teens are going to take risks whether you encourage them or discourage them, and whether you worry yourself sick or you just let them get on with it. So you might as well look positively on their explorations of the world and their own capabilities. (It is better for both *your* health and *their* confidence!)

  If you are struggling to think how you could possibly do this, why not:
  - buy yourself a book of quotations and read and re-read the words of courageous pioneers
  - read autobiographies of adventurers
  - watch films and videos featuring daring feats (with a positive outcome, of course!)
  - dig into your own memory bank and remind yourself of some of the pleasure and excitement you had by taking risks in your teen years!

'It is important to recognize that young people often learn from what, on the surface appear to be unhappy or negative experiences. In resolving not to repeat such experiences, they develop a range of psychosocial skills.'

John C. Coleman and Leo B. Hendry, *The Nature of Adolescence*

■ **Help them to develop risk-management skills** – help your teen to assess the level of potential failure and danger of whatever project they want to take on. Discuss with them ways they might be able to reduce the risks by taking certain actions (for example, obtaining more information, getting extra training or telling someone what they are going to do). Help them also to make back-up plans so that they know what they can and will do should things go wrong. Suggest that they also include some confidence re-building in their contingency plan. For example, reminding themselves of their achievements, or spending time with a friend who thinks they are great, or taking time out to do something, such as a sport or hobby, which they are good at.

■ **Encourage them to become more generally self-protective** – as this book is about ways to build confidence, you could, for example, just dip into it and try out (or try again!) almost any of the tips which I have included. As you know, these range from simple ways to reinforce their self-esteem (see page 53) to instructions on keeping their cool (see pages 121–2) and how to say 'No' in a persistent, assertive manner (see page 110).

Alternatively, the particular situation may warrant you paying for them to attend self-defence classes, arranging for them to meet with a friend who has been to the dangerous place they want to visit, or making an appointment for them to see a family planning counsellor.

■ **Teach them how to maintain their calm in a crisis** – help them to learn and practise relaxation, visualization and positive thinking techniques, to enable them to restore their emotional balance (see Rule 15).

- **Take control of your guilt** – we are more prone to knee-jerking into over-protective responses if we have a reservoir of guilt. I have often heard parents talking about their fear and guilt in virtually the same breath. When we have analysed their response in more detail, it often emerges that it has as much to do with helping them feel better about themselves as it does about protecting their child.

  'I just had to stop him – I was so frightened and I feel so guilty for not knowing what that place had become like. Perhaps if I had taken him there myself, I'd have known. In my day it wasn't that dangerous … But you see, I work so hard all week that on Saturdays I just need to rest.'

  'She's never going to be allowed to do that again … I can't tell you what a fright I had … if only I had warned her. It was my own fault – I just thought she was more mature than that. But there's no way we'll take the risk of trusting her on her own again.'

  A much more constructive way of dealing with your guilt would be to:

  – analyse whether your guilt is rational or irrational: talking through the situation with someone who can be more objective than you is usually a good way to do this

  – if it is rational, say sorry and plan a practical course of action to make amends. For example, if you seriously have omitted to give your child important precautionary information, phone the bookshop or help-line and order copies of what you or they need immediately. For example, you could ring the Drugs Line to obtain leaflets or you could buy a copy of Aidan Macfarlane and Ann McPherson's book called *Teenagers: The Agony, The Ecstasy, The Answers*, which contains useful information and addresses for a whole range of problems. If your guilt still persists, try reading the section on guilt in my book, *Emotional Confidence*. Another of my books, *Success from Setbacks*, might also help you to look at how to turn mistakes into opportunities

- if you know your guilt is irrational, try to discover why you are beating yourself up unnecessarily. For example, if you feel guilty about being neglectful, but the reality is that you do spend as much time as you can with each of your children, it could be that you have let your own self-esteem sink too low. Alternatively, you could be over-stressed and not feeling in full control of yourself and your life. (I hope the remedies for both these ills will be obvious by the time you have finished reading this book!)

- **Take control of your own anxiety** – use and practise the relaxation techniques that I discuss in Rule 15. Divert your attention from what your teen might be doing and your worry about what might happen. Make sure that you have some absorbing activities always at hand.

- **Affirm your trust in them and the outcome** – try not to wave them good-bye with a worried look and dire warnings. Instead, try to convey this kind of message both verbally and non-verbally:
  'I'm sure you'll take care of yourself – you are going to have a great time.'

Rule 14:
Do Battle with the Bullies Both for Them and with Them

'My mum told me to be proud of who I was, lips and all ... now any-time someone says something to me that I find offensive and hurtful, I dig down inside and remember the good things.'

young adult talking about being bullied for her Afro looks

Bullying is currently on the increase not just in schools but in the adult world as well. It used to be a male problem, but now research reveals that girls are just as likely as boys to be bullied and to be bullies themselves. If you are reading this because your child appears to lack confidence, you may have already had some personal experience of it. But even if you haven't had any direct experience, it is possible that your child has, without you knowing anything about the situation.

It is common knowledge that bullies tend to target (though by no means exclusively) those that are generally seen to be weak or 'odd'. This is one of the reasons why, when your children reach their teens, they may choose to suffer their bullying in silence. They do not want to be labelled with either of these traits. Another reason is, of course, they are scared that by divulging what is going on, they will suffer even more hurt and humiliation. So it is not surprising that even when evidence of the bullying does manage to reach adult ears, a teenager will commonly deny it or beg you to keep quiet and do nothing.

Having seen so many unhappy adults whose personalities were undoubtedly damaged by bullying in childhood, you would expect me to take a tough position on this subject. And I do! I am firmly convinced that it is vital that parents act in an authoritative and protective way. I believe it is unequivocally wrong to even expect older teenagers to stand up for themselves by themselves. The reality is that often they can't, and even more often, they won't.

Not only do most teenagers lack the social skills to confront bullies effectively, they do not have enough experience of the world to be able to know the dangers that non-intervention can bring. Without frightening them even more, we have to make them realize that something has to be done to stop the bully. They need to know that even if they find a way of coping, many other vulnerable children (including maybe their younger brothers or sisters) do not. I have listed below some examples of the negative effects which research has revealed results from bullying. Discussing these with your teen will hopefully convince them to allow you to join them in taking some action. If it doesn't, and they are still officially under your care and protection, I hope you will consider taking some kind of action on their behalf. This is especially important if there is a chance that gang bullying is taking place or if the bullying is coming from a teacher or other influential adult such as a sports coach.

Most teenagers do not have the social skills to confront bullies effectively – it is *your* job to join them in taking some action.

Why bullying must be stopped

Here are just a few examples of the possible long-term consequences of ignoring bullying behaviour. Victims are more likely to:

- under-achieve because their self-esteem has been knocked and energy is being wasted on negative emotions such as resentment, guilt and fear
- suffer physical symptoms of stress such as headaches, sickness, muscle tension
- turn their anger inwards and become depressed and cynical
- avoid or cope badly in situations where they meet figures of authority
- over-conform
- become well-practised at hiding their true feelings and therefore less able to have satisfying intimate relationships
- become reclusive and eventually lonely
- hide their talents for fear of creating envy in others
- develop a belief that there is little point in fighting any kind of injustice
- leave other victims to fend for themselves
- become bullies themselves

Bullies are likely to:

- continue bullying throughout their life
- eventually become lonely and socially ostracized
- suffer low self-esteem and inner angst in spite of any external signs to the contrary
- become depressed and cynical about the world and act in accordance with these beliefs
- turn to criminality (a survey in Norway found that 6 out of 10 school bullies had committed an offence by the time they were 24 years old)
- become more angry and/or disillusioned and consequently a serious danger to themselves and/or others

Top Tips

- **Help them to be clear about the line between bullying and teasing** – teasing isn't really meant to be taken seriously and it is not intended to hurt anyone. It is (or should be able to be) a two-way process. Bullying is one-sided and is about one person being nasty at the expense of a weaker person. At its core, it is about hurting and creating fear. In contrast, at the core of teasing is the desire to have mutual fun.

- **Look out for knock-on effects at home** – although your teen may well do a very effective job of covering up their distress when at school or with their friends, there will almost certainly be signs you may be able to spot at home. So keep an eye out for any of the symptoms listed above, plus any others which you think may indicate that they have a problem. Be particularly careful to check out that they are not being bullied themselves if you spot them bullying their younger siblings.

- **Encourage them to take verbal bullying seriously** – the well-known British saying often heard in playgrounds 'Sticks and stones will break my bones, but words can never hurt me' has a lot to answer for in my opinion! The words of bullies, especially when brains are still highly impressionable, can ring in people's ears throughout their lives. They do have enormous power to damage self-esteem and create unnecessary fear and anxiety.

- **Devise together easy-to-remember strategies** – which they can use in the face of bullying. Here is one which I have devised. You could use it for the non-violent (and by far the most common) kind of bullying. You may find that working together you can come up with a more personal or appropriate version.

CAT!
a strategy for responding to a non-violent attack

Have you seen a cat's response when bullied by a dog? They confidently stand their ground, arch their backs, stare at the dog and hiss persistently until he goes away. Their strategy is not fool-proof in the face of all violence from all canine threats, but the vast majority of times it is highly successful.

So in the face of a bullying attack, think: CAT!

Calm confidence – take some deep slow breaths from your stomach to calm your breathing and heart. Adopt a confident stance by standing tall, keeping both feet firmly on the ground and gaining direct eye contact.

Assertive refusal – persistently refuse to do what they are telling you to do. Don't rise to the bait. Instead, just repeat in a calm voice the *same* simple refusal statement over and over again in response to taunts and threats. For example: *'No, I won't do that ... No, I won't do that ... No, I won't do that.'*

This is a well-tried and tested assertive technique. It will prompt the vast majority of bullies to back off, at least temporarily.

Tell the tale – speak to someone, preferably an adult who will deal with the incident with the seriousness that it deserves. Ask them for help. Don't be tempted to 'go it alone again' or keep quiet just because the bully has backed off this time. Bullies have a nasty habit of returning with reinforcements. And if they do not, you can be pretty sure they are busy seeking another victim.

- **Coach them on how to respond to a potentially violent attack** – a worrying trend is that these are becoming more common. In response, more and more teenagers are carrying weapons and creating dangerous vicious cycles. The only sensible thing to do in potentially violent situations is to turn and run as fast as you can and/or scream for help as loudly as you can. Alternatively, if you have given them a sound alarm they could, of course, set this off. But remember, it is not enough to just provide your teen with an alarm, they will need practise in setting it off. They will also need to be encouraged and reminded to take the alarm with them whenever they go out to potentially threatening places.

- **Keep a record of bullying attacks** – authorities such as the school, the police or Social Services are obviously much more likely to take a number of incidents more seriously than one or two.

- **Complain if you don't get the help which you requested** – don't give up if nothing happens when you go to the school or any other organization and discuss the situation. Put a complaint in writing, being careful to stick to facts and leave out your subjective opinion. Take a copy of your letter before sending it off to a higher authority. Don't be afraid to go public with your complaint – bullying is so rife that you will quickly find other people who have had the same experience. If you can persuade your teen to talk to someone else who has been through the same experience, so much the better. You could find this kind of help from the school counselling or mentoring service or from your local youth services department.

- **Take an interest in the anti-bullying policy of their school** – every school in the UK should now have one of these. If your child's school does not have a policy, ask the head teacher if he or she has any plans to develop one. Often nothing happens simply because no one (or not enough people) has jolted anyone into action. The promotion of these kinds of policies can be an effective deterrent. So even if you are not aware of trouble at the moment, give them your support anyway. The fact that you show that you care and campaign for these issues will be a confidence boost in itself for your teen.

- **Give them permission to avoid the bullies** – at least until the situation is sorted. Many children feel that they might lose face by doing this. Emphasize that this is a sensible rather than cowardly course of action. Reinforce their right to choose the company they keep. This is especially important if they have been bullied because they are different in some way. In the harsh reality of the modern world, the chances are that they will be bullied again and again by certain types of people in certain types of organizations. They have a right to lessen their stress in life by choosing to avoid such people.

Rule 15:
Equip Them Efficiently for
Their Emotional Roller Coaster Rides

> 'We should remember that adults often contain their feelings, whereas teenagers tend to act them out more readily; they have a tendency to express them in quite an exaggerated way.'
>
> Jacki Gordon and Gillian Grant

If we could eavesdrop on family life with a teenager, aren't these just a few of the despairing cries we might well hear from parents?

> *'Calm down – don't get so excited'*
> *'Don't shout at me – I've had enough of your temper tantrums'*
> *'Oh, you're in a mood again, are you?'*
> *'Don't be so apathetic – get moving!'*
> *'You're too sensitive – I was only ...'*
> *'You're just too jealous!'*

This is a time when feelings can run riot both externally and internally. It is not just the hormonal changes of puberty that tend to cause the problems. Teenagers are under so much stress and are subject to so many powerful new experiences that they are frequently in a prolonged state of heightened emotion. Is it any wonder that their 'system' crashes from time to time and then they then feel 'nothing' or 'dead'?

Can you remember ever being given any forewarning about this turbulent period before it suddenly hit you? Even if you can, it is pretty unlikely that you were given any advice on how to cope. It is only in very recent years that anyone outside the professional world of therapy has given serious consideration to this need. The very idea that feelings can be 'managed' or that emotional skills can be learned is still news to most people I meet.

As we noted in the *What Exactly is Confidence?* chapter, emotional control is an essential ingredient of confidence. But how can anyone feel or appear self-assured if they are constantly at the mercy of a concoction of chemicals circulating round their bodies?

Thanks in part to all the media attention given to Daniel Goleman's book, *Emotional Intelligence,* during the last few years, an awareness of the importance of emotional skills entered the world of business. Employers are now realizing just how relevant the management of feelings is to their 'bottom line'. Already the most enlightened ones have started to test new recruits to see if they match an acceptable standard. So perhaps one day in the distant future, emotional skills may join the 3 R's as a fundamental part of the school curriculum. In the meantime, however, the ball is well and truly in the parental court. If we don't take responsibility for helping our teens learn these skills, we will not just run the risk of them suffering problems with confidence, we may also be limiting their employment potential.

Most parents have many more skills in this area than they give themselves credit for. The fact you have never attended a course in the subject certainly doesn't mean that you don't deserve the diploma! You may have learned the proverbial hard way. Trial and error lessons in life are probably still the most effective way of acquiring these skills. Unfortunately, however, they are also the most risky way to develop them. Hindsight might have taught you a great deal about anger management if, for example, you shouted at your boss once too often, but you may well have lost your job in the process. Equally, panic attacks during major interviews or presentations often prompt people into learning the art of relaxation, but their nervousness or stressed state will undoubtedly have cost them many opportunities before that time.

> **You can't ask anyone to control their feelings
> if they don't know how to do so!**

Top Tips
- **Help them to understand the physical workings of their emotions** – explaining what happens in their bodies when they have feelings will help them to realize that they can exert some

control. This is not an area that most parents know a good deal about simply because it is only recently that science has been able to enlighten us. If you need to brush up *your* knowledge in this area, there is a chapter in my book, *Emotional Confidence*, on the subject. Alternatively, ask your doctor to explain the working of your emotional system in simple terms. Your teenager should, at the very least, know:

- how the 'fight or flight' stress response works and the damaging effect on our bodies of allowing it to be set off too often and for too long
- how exercise, or the lack of it, can increase or decrease the production of the hormones which spark off our emotional states
- how certain foods and drinks (not to mention drugs!) interact with our emotional system
- how romantic love (as well as sexual attraction) has a physical base. It might be useful for them to know, for example, that the hormones that are produced give us a short-term 'high' and that is why they may sweat, feel 'funny inside' and may also be partially blinded to the darker aspects of the person or the situation.

■ **Inform them about the relationship between their minds and their feelings** – it is particularly important that they realize that their emotional state can affect their ability to learn, as well as to make rational judgements. For example, they should know that:

- although we need a certain amount of anxiety to learn and do our best, too much will affect our capacity to lay down new memories and recall old ones
- being in a negative feeling state means that our brains will tend to deselect positive information and come up with negative solutions to match our emotional state
- while we are in a highly charged emotional state, our logical and analytical reasoning powers are more limited

- feeling deeply about an issue is not the same as having an intuitive idea
- many of our 'auto-feeling' responses are habits which were probably developed at an early age and may not be appropriate in current situations
- feelings can be 'contagious' and our brains can respond to other people's moods without us realizing that this has happened
- we can become physically addicted to the hormones which our bodies produce when we are in a state of high emotional arousal such as anger, fear, excitement or even love.

■ **Ensure that they know how to relax** – you may have to 'shop around' to find the kind of techniques and exercises that work for them. Remember that these may not be *your* favourites. There are now so many books, cassettes and courses on relaxation that this should not be a difficult task. But, in case you haven't the time or opportunity at the moment to do much research, here are the two which I have found work best with most people. You could practise these together with your teen or you could photocopy them and give them to them to try themselves. One of my daughters enjoyed doing relaxations with me, the other wouldn't entertain the idea in a million years!

A basic 20-minute relaxation

This classic method of relaxation is achieved by firstly contracting and then relaxing each of the major muscle groups in turn. This should make you much more aware of the different sensations in your body when your muscles are tensed. If you practise doing this regularly, you will eventually be able to relax your muscles on command. Although this particular method takes some time, it is a good one to choose if you have never experienced a state of deep relaxation before. It is also good if you are very tense or anxious just before an exam, perhaps. Many people also use it when they have difficulty getting off to sleep. (It is the one that most mothers are taught at antenatal classes but it is soon forgotten!)

You can ask someone with a soothing voice to read out the instructions. Alternatively, you could record them yourself onto a tape with your favourite relaxing music or sounds in the background.

Some people work down from the muscles in the top of their heads, others prefer to start with their feet. Try doing it one way several times before reversing the way you start.

Choose a quiet, darkened room (or use eye shades). You can put on a tape or CD of some quiet, relaxing music or rhythmic sounds, but you should also practise being able to do the exercise in silent and noisy environments. Most people find it easier to learn this technique if they are lying down (with arms lying by the side of the body, legs slightly apart), but it is also a good idea to practise it in a sitting position as well.

Now start your relaxation:
- Take three deep, slow breaths. Notice the passage of your breath in and out of your body.
- Now just allow yourself to breathe slowly and easily in a regular rhythm.
- Lift your eyebrows upwards as high as they will go, as you try to tense your scalp muscles, and then relax them.
- Close your eyes tight, as tight as you possibly can. Feel all the tension and then relax them.
- Curl your upper lip up to your nose. Feel the tension, then relax.
- Curl your lower lip down towards your chin. Feel the tension, then relax.
- Curl up your tongue in your mouth, and then relax it.
- Clench your teeth. Feel the tension and then relax them.
- Push your jaw forward and backwards.
Now sense how relaxed and heavy your head is feeling.
- Bend your chin forward to touch your chest. Feel the tension and then relax it. Push your head backwards, as far back as it will go. Feel the tension and then relax it. Turn your head to the left. Feel the tension, then relax. Turn your head to the right. Feel the tension. Relax.

- Shrug your shoulders as high up as they will go. Feel the tension, then relax. Push your shoulder blades back. Feel the tension. Relax. Bring your shoulders forward. Feel the tension. Relax.
- Press your arms into your sides, as tight as you can. Relax. Bend your arms at the elbows. Squeeze as tight as you can. Relax.
- Bend your wrists backwards as far as they will go. Relax.
- Clench your hands as tight as you can. Relax.

Focus again on your breathing – in ... out ... in ... out. Check that the muscles you have worked on are still relaxed.

- Now pull your stomach in as tight as you can. Relax.
- Contract your anal muscles and your pelvic floor as tightly as you can. Relax.

Now sense how relaxed and heavy the whole upper part of your body is feeling. If you notice that any muscle is still not relaxed, just tighten and relax it a couple of times again.

- Bring your left knee to your chest as tightly as you can. Relax.
- Bring your right knee to your chest as tightly as you can. Relax.
- With bent knees, press both knees together as tightly as you can. Relax.
- Bend your heels backwards as far as you can. Relax.
- Stretch your feet forward as tight as you can. Relax.
- Curl your toes up as tight as you can. Relax.

Now focus on your breathing once again – in and out.

- Imagine yourself lying on some soft sand on a warm beach.
- Hear the waves gently breaking in the background.
- Be aware of some wispy clouds floating across the deep blue sky.
- Allow your body to feel heavier and heavier.
- Let your mind float as though it was moving away from your body.
- Enjoy this deeply relaxed sensation for a further few moments.

Slowly bring your attention back into the room and take a few deep breaths before opening your eyes. Start to move your body gently and slowly when you sense your energy returning.

A quick visualization technique

Choose a scene that has peaceful memories for you. This could be your favourite holiday place, a room at home, or a quiet corner of your favourite bar where a couple of close friends are sitting.

Before starting the relaxation, use your imagination to take you on a detailed 'tour' around this scene. It may help to have a photograph of your scene to remind you of its details. Notice an object, which is about midway through your tour. When I do this exercise, I visualize our garden in Spain and I focus on a beautiful fountain as the midway point in my tour. You will be using this same scene over and over again because you will be training your brain to instantly switch off its stress response the moment you recall this scene.

Try and practise this relaxation at least twice a day even when you are not particularly stressed. You can do it when you are hanging around waiting for someone or when you are sitting in a bus or a train. The more often you do it, the quicker your brain will respond when you need to look or be relaxed. It will also keep you free of muscle tension, which eats up energy and can bring on headaches and stomach upsets.

Now start your relaxation.
- Sit or stand in a relaxed, well-supported position. (Both feet slightly apart on the ground and with loose hands and arms.)
- Close your eyes and visualize your scene.
- As you breathe in, use your mind's eye to travel gently to your mid-way point and then, as you breathe out, complete the second half of your tour until you come back to your starting point again.
- Repeat several times until you sense your body and mind have relaxed.

■ **Teach them how to generate positive emotion** – attacks of the blues, apathy and zero confidence are common occurrences for most teens. Most will pass within a few days, if not hours.

Sometimes the minor triggers are obvious and also unavoidable at their age. I am sure you can recall diving into a black mood purely because you had 'nothing to wear', or a spot had surfaced, or you received an unusually low grade for an exam. Maybe you can also recall they had a habit of coming at thoroughly inconvenient times, such as prior to a party or set of exams. Explain that (unless they are seriously depressed or in a state of grief) they can stimulate their brains to produce more energizing adrenalin or 'happy hormones' (endorphins and serotonin). Suggest some everyday ways that they may be able to do this. (They may be obvious to you but not necessarily to them.) For example:

- playing uplifting music or running it silently through your head while visualizing one of your favourite places
- doing some strenuous aerobic exercise or sport – or just on-the-spot marching if there is little time
- making a special portable photo album of favourite people and keeping it always at hand
- soaking yourself in an aromatic, oily or bubbly bath with a book, music and a couple of special chocolates
- watching humorous videos

Encourage them to develop their own favourite methods, so they will train their brain to instantly recognize them.

Alternatively, you could teach them the following technique. It is a tried and tested one now used widely in the world of business. It was developed by NLP (the Neuro Linguistic Programming movement) and is similar in its method to the scenic visualization above. The main difference is that it makes a neural link in the brain between a small movement and a positive mood. It may take them a little practise to learn, but it will be one they can use for the rest of their lives. Again, you may want to just photocopy the instructions and let them try it out for themselves.

Anchoring – a technique for rekindling positive feelings

This is a simple self-help technique that is now commonly taught in the world of business and sport. In essence, its 'trick' is to enable us to use past experiences of relaxation to instantly access the same positive feeling. It does this by training our brain to make a link between the feeling of our past experience and a particular word, sound or small movement. We can then physically regenerate the same positive mood whenever we say 'the word' or sound, or make its associated physical movement.

Once you have learned how to 'anchor' peaceful, relaxed feelings in your brain, you will also be able to use the same method to summon up other kinds of positive feelings such as self-confidence or excitement. So it certainly is a technique that is worth trying.

The five steps
1. *RELAX* – use your favourite relaxation technique to get yourself into a deeply relaxed (but still conscious!) state.

2. *RECALL* – in as much vivid detail as possible, an experience from the past which helped you to feel calm and at peace. Use your

imagination to 'relive' the experience physically and emotionally. Recall the experience of your senses.

See the colours, shapes and positive facial expressions. Hear all the sounds of the scene. Imagine yourself touching some of the objects in the scene and feel the various textures.

3. *RELIVE* – spend a few minutes enjoying the feelings that accompanied this experience. Now heighten the feeling and make yourself sense it as deeply as you can. Notice what was happening (or not happening!) in your body.

4. *ANCHOR* – while holding onto your intensified feelings, say a particular word (for example, *calm / relax / cool*) or make a small movement. This could be touching a part of your body or moving a limb in a certain kind of way. (For example, putting two particular fingertips together or gently tapping your thigh twice.) If you use a movement, make sure that it is discreet enough to repeat in public without anyone noticing. Some people use a word and a movement together.

5. *REPEAT* – steps three and four several times before bringing yourself gently back into the real world.

Try to practise this exercise as many times as you can over the following few weeks. You will know when you have successfully 'anchored' your resource state in your brain, when just doing your movement or saying your word seems to give you an immediate sense of calm. You will then know you are ready to try your anchor in real-life situations. The more often you use it, the more powerful and useful it will be.

You could note down the five steps on a small card and take it around with you for a while. You can then practise your anchoring whenever you have a spare few moments. Depending on how easy it is for you to take yourself into a deeply relaxed state, it could take from eight to twelve weeks to master the technique. If it still hasn't worked by then, try a different memory, movement or word.

■ **Be aware of the warning signals of potentially serious emotional problems** – although the self-help methods described above can be very effective, no quick-fix technique can be expected to work if a serious depression or deep self-esteem problems have begun to set in. In such cases you need to encourage your teen to take more long-term help from a professional counsellor or doctor. I have listed below some symptoms which may indicate that the problem has become more serious.

Warning signals

Strongly encourage them to seek a check-up with a doctor or a professional counsellor or therapist if you spot any of the following:

1. obsessional or phobic behaviour – to a degree which prevents them from doing what they want or need to do. (Many teens go through mild phases of obsessions and phobias – it is either part of their self-discovery process or in response to the extra stress they are under)
2. sleep disturbance – on a regular basis (especially early morning waking)
3. eating problems – resulting in constant fluctuation in weight or serious loss or gain of weight
4. self-harm – such as cutting or burning their body or taking minor overdoses of any kind of drug (to 'blank it all out')
5. withdrawal – spending so much time alone that his or her relationships with family and friends are seriously suffering. Consistently refusing social invitations which you think they would normally enjoy
6. violence – towards people or objects
7. under-achievement – persistently achieving much lower grades than expected

8. hallucinations – apparently answering voices as if someone has spoken to them when there is no one around

For further advice, consult the school or youth counselling service or your local mental health charity. Most charities for young people now have confidential helplines or web sites. A listing of their up-to-date numbers and addresses can be obtained from library information services or the Internet.

Managing Anger

■ **Reflect on your own ability to express anger safely and constructively and then teach them some skills**. I can't believe that any family can go through the teenage years without anger becoming an issue at some point. As we have already noted, it is a time when frustration and conflict are inevitable and emotions surface very easily. And, of course, it is not just the teens that find their anger becomes a problem, it is parents as well. These sad 'confessions' are more ordinary than extraordinary. I know they reflect the fears, if not the experience of many.

Bob is a marketing executive with two children, one of whom is Tom, aged 15.

'I don't understand what is happening to me. I have never been like this before. Of course the kids irritated me before and I might have shouted at them from time to time. But my wife always said I had more patience than she did. Now I seem to be flaring up all the time ... sometimes I feel I might actually hurt him, I get so mad. He just winds me up so much. We used to be so close but now all he seems to want from me is money ... Well, yes, I suppose I am exaggerating ... but he makes me so angry ... an example? Well, last Saturday he flew into a toddler tantrum just because I asked him for the tenth time to remove his boots from the centre of the lounge. Well, I just snapped. I told him to get out of the house – he stormed out swearing. Then, of course, I spend half the night scouring

the streets looking for him. I was worried sick. We just continually rub each other up the wrong way and we've both got a hell of a temper, I suppose.'

Julia is a part-time shop assistant and mother of three girls. Lucy, her middle daughter, has recently turned 13 years old.

'She's always flying into rages over the slightest thing – she can't find her tights; her sister's music is too loud, she's got too much homework – it can be anything. I tell her she's making me ill – she just gives me a mouthful ... What do I do then? ... Well, I've given up trying to punish her – it's no good. I just go off and have a cig and a coffee and try to drown out her racket upstairs with the TV. Yes, my migraines are a lot worse, every other day now. The doctor says I should try anti-depressants ... I know she doesn't mean half of what she says but it hurts me. She is always sorry afterwards and at heart I know she's a real softie like me. She says she doesn't mean to hurt me, she just doesn't know how to stop herself. I suppose its just a teenage phase ... do you think she'll grow out of it? I'm worried because she's always falling out with her friends as well.'

Before even beginning to help their teenagers with any of their anger problems, Bob and Julia both have to deal first with their *own* lack of control. Luckily they realized that their teens' short fuses had sparked off an unhelpful response from them and they sought help. Their reactions were, of course, stereotypical. Bob, as a man, became overly angry himself and Julia became depressed. But, of course, it could have been the other way around.

Anger management is not something that any of us can learn quickly or easily, especially if our bad habits are well entrenched. But I know from having to work on my own fiery temperament that it is possible to learn to express frustration and even rage in a safe and assertive manner. Thank goodness I had done this work (and written my book, *Managing Anger*) before my girls went through their teens. So, even if I was not always able to play my anger 'by my own book',

I did know where I was going wrong. This meant that I could apologize for the times I mishandled my anger and initiate a talk on what we could both have said or done differently. This wisdom did not keep our home entirely tantrum or mood-free, but I am sure that our après-anger talks brought us closer together and taught us a great deal about ourselves.

> 'Don't condemn me, but think of me as a person who sometimes reaches bursting point!'
>
> Anne Frank

In the following box, I have listed three main styles of expressing anger. If you are able to model the assertive way for 70% of the time and effectively repair the damage of the other 30%, expressed either passively or aggressively, you will be a perfect example for your teen! There is a time and place for using all three styles. Knowing that we have the freedom and ability to choose between these, depending on the situation, boosts our sense of inner security.

Once you feel reasonably confident that *you* understand how to express anger in an assertive way and know how to defuse sudden flare-ups, start talking to your teenager. Don't wait until they are in the midst of an outburst or have just trashed their sister's best boots in anger. One form of rage or other is always being talked about in the media nowadays so there will be plenty of opportunity. TV soaps are full of examples of mismanaged anger! You could, of course, show the following guidelines to an older teenager or simplify them for a younger one. The next time anyone in the family expresses their anger badly (and someone usually will!) conduct a post-mortem and discuss together how the situation could have been handled differently by all parties concerned. Resist the temptation to just 'kiss and make-up' or 'sweep the incident under the carpet'. Treat these real-life experiences as golden opportunities to learn. The ideal place to learn anger skills is a safe environment surrounded by people who love you in spite of the devil inside you.

Finally, a word of warning! If anyone in your family uses an aggressive anger style repeatedly, seek professional help immediately. The sooner this kind of habit is nipped in the bud, the less likely it is to escalate into violent behaviour.

And don't forget that an over-reliance on the passive style can also be dangerous. It can lead to self-destructive and depressive habits, which can be hard to break once they are entrenched.

Anger is a natural, protective response to frustration and threat. Used safely and constructively, it is a powerful tool for righting injustice and changing bad practice.

Three possible ways to handle anger

1. The PASSIVE Way
This is when we do not express our feelings openly. Instead, we 'bottle them up' or 'swallow them'.

You can often spot the non-verbal signs more easily than the words, which may be polite and non-angry. Look for tightened muscles such as pursed lips, crossed arms and legs, slight eye-closing and also small body-damaging habits such as biting fingers or lips, digging into, banging or scratching one's own body and blinking and swallowing to fight back tears.

Its advantages:

- It will temporarily keep the peace: it can enable us to carry on what we may need or want to do. (For example, to continue watching the film, taking in information or enjoying the party.)
- It can protect us from violence because it is not perceived as threatening. (The other person's 'fight or flight' response does not switch on because its body signals do not set it off.)
- It can give us some breathing space to plan or get support. We can prepare more carefully what we want to say, or do, to put right the injustice or relieve our frustration. We can gather information and

back-up support which might strengthen our chances of winning.
- It can be useful in negotiations: these require us to look calm and reasonable and stay focused on the agenda.

Its disadvantages:

- It is tempting to keep the anger suppressed for too long; we may then 'chicken out' of confronting the situation or simply forget it.
- Excessive tension will also begin to build in our body. Repressing anger frequently causes stress symptoms such as headaches, stomach disorders and other aches and pains. If we do this regularly, we will begin to suffer both mentally and emotionally. When anger is continually forced inwards and allowed to fester it can lead to depression or obsessive and self-destructive behaviour (such as drinking too much, eating too little, or driving too fast).
- We may find ourselves 'getting our own back' in indirect ways. (For example, secretly manipulating situations so that the offending person is hurt or let down / spreading malicious gossip behind their backs or giving them public put-downs / trashing or not bothering to look after the world around us.)
- In the long-term, our relationships almost always suffer: hidden resentment leads to unpleasant 'atmospheres' and picking quarrels. It also makes it difficult for people to trust each other or interact spontaneously. (This is one of the most common reasons why relationships suddenly and unexpectedly cool.)
- There is also the danger that innocents will become victims: the 'steam' of past frustrations is often vented at 'targets' who have less power or people we know we can trust. (For example, younger brothers or sisters or our best friend can take the flack deserved by someone else.)
- There is a danger someone will get hurt; repressed anger can suddenly leak out to anyone at any time, especially when we are under pressure or are over-tired. Someone might say or do something which acts as the 'last straw' without realizing that they are doing so. There is always the danger that this could be someone who has

real power to hurt. In their surprised state, they could respond to this unfair 'attack' aggressively or violently.

2. The AGGRESSIVE Way

This is when we respond with threatening, destructive, hurtful or bullying behaviour.

It is usually easy to recognize. The words used tend to be accusatory and insulting. The angry person is likely to raise their voice, glare, sneer, move forward and wave their arms in a threatening manner. Even if our mind misses these signals, our bodies won't. They will respond automatically with a 'fight or flight' response.

Its advantages:

- It can frighten off *some* threats (for example, cowardly or surprised bullies).
- Our displeasure, irritation and dissatisfaction cannot be missed even if it is ignored.
- We release some of the tension in our bodies that anger produces.

Its disadvantages:

- The other person can become angry or frightened. They may then run away literally or mentally (by 'switching-off') or they could start a fight.
- Objects and/or the environment can be damaged or destroyed. If we cannot hit the offending person, we often lash out at something else.
- We can frighten off potential support. Few people like to get caught in the crossfire, so even those who think you are right to be angry might keep quiet. (An 'army' usually stands a better chance of winning than a lone guerrilla does.)
- We don't see the opportunities. Aggressive anger puts our brain into a negative mode, so our eyes and ears might not notice if someone is backing down, saying sorry, or offering a good way of making amends.

– We can lose the respect or trust of people we value; no amount of 'sorrys' can wipe away some memories. Upfront aggressive behaviour terrifies many people and is considered unforgivable in certain cultures, organizations or families.

3. *The ASSERTIVE way*

This is when we use words to express our feelings calmly and straight-forwardly. Our bodies are held in a calm, confident pose. If someone appears to be to blame for the selfish behaviour, hurt, injustice or threat we will tell them and say what changes we want, while at the same time taking responsibility for our own emotional response. You can say, for example:

'You have just interrupted me again. I am beginning to feel angry, so I need to calm myself down before I can talk any more about it.'
rather than:

 'Shut-up – you're making me angry, do you want to make me ...' (aggressive) or, *'Okay, if that's how you want it. I won't utter another word.'* (passive)

'I become irritated when I hear you two arguing constantly. I would like you both to ...'
rather than:

'Stop that row. Your constant bickering is driving me mad. Any more of it and I will ...' (aggressive) or, *'I've got a headache. I'm going upstairs.'* (passive)

Its advantages:

– People don't feel cornered and are less likely to react defensively. They feel they have the choice whether to continue or not with the behaviour which has triggered anger.
– It stimulates a thinking or verbal response rather than an emotional or physical one. There is less chance that they will become immedi-ately 'inflamed' with anger themselves.
– It reduces the possibility of misunderstandings because the anger is expressed directly to the person concerned and clear, non-inflammatory language is used.

– Trust and respect is strengthened because everyone knows where they stand and most people respect honesty even if they may not like what they hear.

Its disadvantages:

– It may not be heard, especially if the other person is overly angry, stressed or pre-occupied, or is a hardened bully.
– Where there is great instability, it can make matters worse. If the boat is too fragile to be rocked, it will collapse – if there is no other means to get to shore, everyone sinks! So some very weak people and rocky relationships cannot take the strain of the slightest criticisms or whiff of ill feeling.
– It may take too long to get a response. If the situation is dangerous, anger expressed aggressively will usually demand instant attention and stimulate prompt action. (For example, if someone is physically hurting you or anyone else, your immediate need is to stop them – you can't afford the time to talk!)

How to defuse your anger

Use this strategy as soon as you feel your own anger beginning to take a hold in your body. You may notice that your pulse is quickening or your stomach muscles are tightening or your finger is tapping. In taking each of the following steps you are, in effect, sending 'switch-off' signals to the 'fight or flight' centre in your emotional brain.

The first letters of each word in the sentence 'Don't Get Too Boiling' are the same as the first letters of each of the steps. Memorize it as soon as you can.

Don't	**Get**	**Too**	**Boiling**
I	R	E	R
S	O	N	E
T	U	S	A
A	N	I	T
N	D	O	H
C		N	E
E			

Step 1: Distance – immediately let go of any physical contact with objects (possible fighting tools!). Take a step back or lean back in a chair.

   If you have the time, leave the room for a while or 'sleep on it' before expressing your feelings.

Step 2: Ground – now 'earth' your body by putting both feet firmly on the ground and holding on to some firm stationary object. Then bring your mind 'back down to earth' by giving it a mundane activity such as counting backwards from 10 or 50, or counting all the blue objects you can see around you.

   If you have more time, do some chore or activity which will distract you temporarily from what has made you angry.

Step 3: Tension – next, release tension by clenching and unclenching some of your muscles. You could clench and unclench fists; screw your face up and/or curl and uncurl your toes.

   If you have the time, unwind yourself further by doing some strenuous physical activity or sport.

Step 4: Breathe – finally, take one or two deep slow breaths for at least the next five minutes.

   If you have the time, do a relaxation exercise which demands controlled breathing such as meditation or yoga.

And Finally ...

■ **Encourage them to enjoy their emotions** – feelings can be so problematic during these years that is very easy for some teens who lack confidence to become quite frightened by this side of themselves. As a result, they may try to 'deaden' themselves by throwing themselves into their academic work or becoming overly sober and serious about issues. They may pride themselves on being 'cool' and unmoved by 'sentimentality'. They might start scorning you for showing any kind of passion or sentiment and become annoyingly cynical and pedantic.

Rather than confronting them head on with this kind of defensive behaviour (which often makes it worse), encourage them to do more of the activities which you know can spark off their excitement, sense of fun or compassion.

You can also try hinting at what they might be feeling. For example: *'If that happened to me, I'd be quite upset'* / *'That sounds exciting'* / *'I remember when I took my first oral exam, I felt ...'*

So, while it is important to give them the skills to control their feelings when they need to, it is equally important to give them lots of 'permission' to be emotionally free and spontaneous, especially in the safe haven of their home.

Aim to make your home a safe haven for your teen to both feel and express every kind of emotion.

Rule 16:
Coach as well as Comfort Them Through Their Relationship Crises

> 'As young adolescents mature, they become dissatisfied with cliques and crowds and they begin to seek out close friends ... Intense attachments form much more quickly at this age than at any other ... but these relationships can disintegrate quickly.'
>
> Laura Sessions Stepp

Relationships probably hurt more during our teen years than at any other stage in our lives. It is a time when friendship and love is frequently pushed to its limits. There is also heightened awareness of the human capacity to hurt, hate and control. It can be a toughly competitive time and is commonly full of dramatic falling ins and outs.

In the relationship game, it is the confident children who are undoubtedly the winners. They are the sought-after friends, the adventurous lovers and the kings of the gangs. Amongst peers, success in relationships is probably an even more important way of gaining status than achieving great grades or even scoring the goals.

I have heard many parents lament over how hard it is to watch their less confident children go through these testing times. They often feel powerless and say that all they feel they can do is watch and wait and then 'be there for them' when the inevitable crises occur. They talk with each other about how tough it is to see them making the same mistakes as they made and not be able to prevent them from getting hurt.

Of course, much of what they are saying is true. Most relationship skills are learned through real-life practise. Most of the time we have to just sit back and let our children play the field and take the risks. But once they do encounter problems we are back in the scene once again. And we can do so much more than just give them a cuddle and cheer them up. We can use the crises as an opportunity to help them learn social survival know-how and rebuild their confidence.

There are of course exceptions to this rule. Sometimes, we have to try to pre-empt possible hurt because the risks are too great. For example, we may have information or a strong intuitive feeling that there is danger ahead. Or, we may be fairly certain that there is a chance that they could get pregnant or physically assaulted, or be seduced into breaking the law. In these situations, of course, they need clear warnings and possibly restrictions – even if they give us 'grief' and plenty of attitude in return!

Top Tips

- **If they complain that they have no friends, don't waste your energy trying to convince them they are wrong** – this is a common cry from teenagers and the crisis has often miraculously vanished by the following morning. Just listen attentively to their story and feelings (see Rule 3) and wait for a few days. Then, if the concern doesn't appear to have vanished, suggest an activity that you can do together which will allow you to comfortably raise the subject again. Help them to 'diagnose' the cause of the problem and give them some of your wisdom by asking indirect questions and sharing, rather than probing and giving head-on advice. For example:

  'I was thinking about what you told me on Tuesday and wondering if the friends you have been making are the right ones for you. I know I've grown out of friends sometimes – the trouble is we can change and then we want different things from friends ...'

  Even if your guesses about the nature of the problem are wrong, you may stimulate them into disclosing or clarifying what the real issue is.

- **Encourage and coach them on how to start new friendships** – many teens are simply not very skilled at starting up conversations. I also regularly meet adults who confess to having the same problem and often trace it back to their teenage years. Sadly, they have usually spent years avoiding situations where this skill is needed. As a result, they are often 'trapped' in friendships that have long ago passed their sell-by-date. When they were teenagers, their parents may not even have noticed their lack of skill in making new friends simply because they may not have seen them in the situations where it would have been apparent.

The good news is that this is one of those confidence problems that is very easy to put right. You can, for example, help them prepare a few opening small talk (or even chat-up!) lines and then take them to social situations where they can practise these safely. (Holidays provide a great opportunity for this.) You can also warn them about getting too personal too quickly and give them some pointers on how to wind down conversations if they want to move on. There are also many books on the subject that could be very helpful. I have listed some in my *Further Help* section at the end of the book.

The important message to get across is that there is no 'magic' involved. They need to know that these kinds of skills have to be learned at some time by *everyone* – even if some of us learn them more easily than others. Give them examples of people who were once shy and now socialize comfortably. Celebrity interviews and autobiographies often reveal early difficulties in this area. (Actors often go into their business to get over their shyness). You may also have some good examples nearer home as well. Perhaps a family member they know will talk about this as a past problem. I have known older brothers and sisters to be of great help.

Another easy way you can show them how it is done is by pointing out examples of good and bad 'chat-up' scenes when you are watching TV together. You'll be spoilt for choice in the popular soaps!

Finally, I hope that by now it goes without saying that you must also be an inspiring example! Make sure that you frequently invite new acquaintances to your home and take them often to places where neither of you know anyone. (New holiday destinations, for example.) This will give them some real-life demonstration, as well as a chance for them to practise. Don't forget to praise them when they have done well.

- **Help them feel comfortable with being disliked and rejected by *some* people** – this is a hard one! What loving parent feels comfortable when their child is disliked or rejected? My initial reaction to anyone who didn't think my girls were irresistibly wonderful was always highly defensive. To say that I couldn't find a good word to say about these people is a gross understatement. Part of me hated them! So you may also find that before you can convince your teen that being disliked by someone is not the greatest tragedy, you may have to remind yourself that there really are plenty of other nice fish in the sea.

- **Tell them how they can assert themselves when they are treated with disrespect**. Accepting the fact that we are disliked or have been rejected by someone doesn't mean that we also have to tolerate disrespectful behaviour towards ourselves. Indeed, we do not have to accept it even from people we like or love. These are both critical confidence-building messages to convey.

But we need to do more than be indignant on their behalf. We should teach them how to stand up for this right without compromising their values and their dignity. If, for example, they have been put-down, don't just give them sympathy and curse the bad guys. Help them work out an assertive comeback strategy. If that is not possible, rehearse with them what they could say in response next time. Photocopy my guidelines in the box below. Give them a copy and talk it through with them.

Dealing with put-downs

Put-downs are remarks or actions which are *intentionally* used to make the other person feel 'small'. It is important to remember that sometimes they are disguised as 'nice' behaviour. This is why we often don't realize until after the event that we have been put-down. The penny drops later when we start to feel bad and we realize that the compliment was a back-hander after all. Alternatively, someone else may open our eyes to the truth. A good friend who has witnessed the put-down might say, 'Why did you put up with him saying that to you?' The put-down may have passed you by at the time.

Most put-downs do not come from serious inveterate bullies; they come either from people who do not realize that they are hurting you or from the cowards with petty axes to grind. But their remarks can still erode our self-esteem and our reputation if we do not deal with them assertively. Here are some tips:

1. *Reveal the put-down in its true colours* – if someone asks an apparently innocent question or makes a seemingly nice remark, but you suspect it has a nasty undertone, check it out. Using an assertive, confident tone of voice, invite a direct criticism. This will

usually take the wind out of their sails pretty quickly and make them much less likely to give any more put-downs. For example:

The put-downer: *'So that's the latest style in tee-shirts, is it?'*
You: *'I like this tee-shirt, but are you saying that it doesn't suit me or that you don't like it?'*
The put-downer: *'Well, no ... it's OK, I suppose.'*

2. **Don't be shy about dealing with the put-down after the event** – even if you were not able to give an immediate assertive answer, you can deal with it later. It is often a good idea to give yourself some thinking time – you can come up with a better defence and prepare yourself emotionally. For example, the next time you see them you can say:

'I have been thinking about that remark you made about my tee-shirt. I was a bit taken aback and hurt at the time. I had just bought that tee-shirt and I like it ...'

3. **Prepare assertive responses to common put-downs** – you can make a list on your own, but it is much more supportive (and fun) to do this with someone else. It helps to identify possible passive and aggressive answers as well. For example:

The 'nagging' style: *'Haven't you told him yet?'*

Passive response: *'I'm awful, aren't I?'*
Aggressive retort: *'Mind your own business.'*
Assertive response: *'No, I haven't. I'll decide myself when the moment is right.'*

The 'questioning your judgement' style: *'That'll never fit you'*

Passive response: *'I suppose you're right.'*
Aggressive retort: *'You're not perfect yourself either – at least I haven't got ...'*
Assertive response: *'I can decide what looks OK on me ... And less of the put-downs, please.'*

The 'sarcastic' style: *'So that's art, is it?'*

Passive response: *'I know it's not very good, but I was trying.'*
Aggressive retort: *'Could you do better yourself?'*
Assertive Response: *'I consider it art. I'd like your opinion, but I find that kind of sarcastic remark insulting. I'd prefer you tell me in a straightforward way what you think I could change.'*

- **If the relationship is sexual, check that they are informed** – even if you have had the birds and bees talk many years ago. For the last few years they may have affected to know 'everything' about such matters. It isn't, however, until they begin to 'play the field' that the gaps in their knowledge begin to become apparent. It is then that they may begin to worry and lose confidence in this area. Under-confident teens are in a vulnerable position because they are typically pretending to be more street-wise than they actually are.

  As much as you might like to help, many teens find sexual talk very embarrassing to have with their parents. This can be disconcerting, especially if you have chatted openly about intimate matters in the past either with them or with your other children. Rather than forcing the issue, remind them that you are happy to talk about *any* problem they may have at *any* time. Share your understanding that it might be difficult for them to talk with you. Provide them with one or two good books or leaflets and the addresses of clinics where they can get confidential free advice.

  Also, rather than force-feeding them with morality tales, express your trust in them. Say that you have every confidence in them that they will look after themselves and that they will ask for help and advice if they find they need it.

- **Be clear where your loyalties lie** – we often become very involved, if not very fond, of our teens' close friends at this age. It can be traumatic for us too when there is a big falling-out and we are threatened with losing contact with one of their friends. It can be particularly difficult if we see the other teen as a child who needs more parenting than they are actually receiving. (Be warned! Children of parents who are dedicated enough to read parenting books have a habit of collecting such friends!)

  Of course, we need to make sure that our children are sensitive to the needs of others who are less fortunate than themselves. But forcing them to continue friendships they do not want is not the way to do this. Often 'difficult' and disturbed children make a 'bee-line' for their less confident peers. Partly because they may lack emotional nourishment themselves, they can be very demanding and hurtful within these relationships while being as sweet as pie with the parents! It is our job to give our children tips on how to assert themselves with such friends and give them our 'blessing' should they want to cool the relationships.

  Similarly, you may need to watch your loyalties if their friend or lover is of the opposite sex and you haven't had a child from that gender of your own. I remember being very excited when boys started to enter our home. They became the sons I never had. I was quite shocked when I found myself over-defending them during their quarrels with my daughters.

  It is hard enough for children with problems of confidence to stand up for themselves and break off relationships without their parents making them feel guilty for doing so! Don't assume that your child knows that ultimately they are the most important person to you during these difficult times. Tell them loud and clear because inside their self-esteem is probably quaking and needs some bolstering.

■ **Teach them about emotional healing** – although this is a
very natural process, nowadays it hardly ever seems to get a
chance to run its course. Perhaps the pace of life is partly to
blame. We want instant emotional cures as well as instant
everything else. Traditionally, within male teen culture it is often
not considered 'cool' to be broken-hearted for long, but today
many girls feel this pressure as well. Watch out for signs that they
are 'papering over' emotional wounds and rushing too quickly
into new relationships.

It may help to motivate them to look after themselves if you
explain the stages of the healing process. Sometimes, for practical
reasons, in the immediate aftermath of their hurt, they may just
have to get on with their life. There may be schoolwork or a
match to play. But they need to know that, eventually, if they
want to restore their emotional resilience they will need to revisit
the hurt and work through the stages I suggest in the following
box.

If their hurt is very deep, or it has rekindled some old
emotional pain, you may need to steer them in the direction of a
counsellor. This is especially true if you yourself are feeling deeply
as well. This is often the case when a rejection from a friend or a
boyfriend reopens an old separation wound made by a divorced or
deceased parent. (And this happens very frequently at this age.)

Should they be reluctant to see a counsellor, or you yourself
think that such a move is an 'over-kill' response, suggest someone
else who might be able to help. This could be another relative
(grandparents often come into their own during these crises) or a
close friend of yours whom they trust. Alternatively, try to steer
them in the direction of one of their friends or an acquaintance
that has been through a similar experience.

Take comfort from the fact that the wisdom they acquire about
emotional healing through these crises will stand them in good
stead for the rest of their life. The recovery process is more or less
the same for every emotional hurt that we encounter, including
significant bereavements and major disappointments. It is not a

'subject' that can ever be taught effectively at school. Certainly it is hard to teach theoretically. Most people need to be hurting before they will even want to learn. As parents, we are in an ideal position to help. I hope the following steps will be a useful guide and reminder for both you and your teen.

How to heal from emotional hurt

Step 1: Think and Talk – about what has happened. Don't push it from your mind and try to pretend or forget that it has happened. Make yourself face it by talking it over or re-living the memories.

Step 2: Feel the Feeling – find a place where you can safely let go of at least some of your emotion. This could be a mixture of feelings such as sadness, disappointment and anger. Music and old photos can help bring these alive.

Step 3: Care with Comfort – ensure that you have plenty of extra rest and nutritional food. Let other people look after you and take all the cuddles you can get.

Step 4: Restore by Recompense – find a way to give yourself some compensation for being hurt. A good time for treats and being with special friends.

Step 5: Vary the View – now (and not before!) is the time to look at what has happened from a positive rather than negative angle. Think about what you have learned and all the good experiences you may have had as well as the hurt. Talk to other people who may be able to look at what has happened, or the other person, from a different perspective. It also sometimes helps to talk to people who have been through the same experience and are now recovered.

Rule 17:
Respond to Their Desire for
Solitude and Secrecy with Tact

> 'I found it satisfying to confide in my diary, as many teenagers do. But to protect myself, in case, God forbid – my mother ever found it, I invented code words so that she would not know what I was talking about.'
>
> Judy Blume

I found this rule so much harder to put into practise than I ever thought I would. Of course I accepted it in theory. After all, I knew that research has shown that in order to promote their maturity, adolescents need a fair degree of solitude. I accepted that it is quite natural for them to retreat to their own rooms for long periods and become more secretive, and sometimes even lie about their activities. I could even remember how important privacy and secrecy had been to me at this age.

But when my daughter, Laura, actually asked at the age of 15 for a lock on her bedroom door, I was shocked!

Firstly, I was hurt. How could she think we would abuse her privacy? I had never looked through her papers or rifled through her drawers and was sure I would never find myself ever tempted to do so. (I had been so angry when that kind of thing had happened to me when I was a teen. I had longed for privacy so much myself, especially during my time in children's homes).

Secondly, I was frightened. What was she trying to hide? Could it be drugs? Could it be something 'dangerous' to do with sex?

Then I found myself thinking of every reason under the sun why it was impractical and even dangerous to have one room in the house locked. What would we do if there was a fire? What would happen if she was ill and we didn't know? Would we get an infestation of mice if she left food around? Would her room *ever* be cleaned? And so forth!

Fortunately, I didn't share my anxieties with Laura. Instead, I talked it through with my husband. Doing this helped me to take control of my defensive response. We both agreed that her request was understandable, even though we considered it unnecessary. We decided that we had to show our trust in her and demonstrate that we respected her right to privacy. So we told Laura that of course she could have a lock fitted. We asked her just to let us know when we should arrange for a locksmith to come.

Interestingly, that was the end of the story. She never asked for the lock to be fitted. We assumed that it was probably enough for her to know that we had said 'Yes' to her request. She had had her right to privacy confirmed and knew that if ever she needed it, she could have it.

But, of course, the incident was a very salutary lesson for me. It made me realize how over-protective of Laura I had become. I am sure that her request for a lock was an indirect message saying, 'Lay-off, mum. I need some space!' (Children will usually tell us in one way or other what they need from us, but how often do we really listen to the messages – especially those we don't want to hear?!)

Top Tips

- **Give them as much secure individual space in your home as you can** – if you can't provide a separate bedroom, find a way of screening off their 'corner' and give them lockable drawers and files or cupboard.

- **Hand over full responsibility of their space to them** – this means they can decide when to tidy or clean it as well as choosing its décor. In spite of our fears, most teens usually do find what they need amongst the clutter and their rooms rarely do become a public health hazard. Also, the vast majority of teenagers do eventually grow into responsible house-proud adults!

- **Make sure you have a lockable bathroom** – this may never have been an issue in your house until this time. I can't tell you why, but sometimes the change seems to happen overnight and can feel hard to take. The child whom you potty trained and who romped naked with you around the house suddenly becomes embarrassed even when you are watching them clean their teeth.

If you have the means to provide them with their own bathroom facilities you can try that option, though I have to admit that it didn't work for us. Our main bathroom was still preferred and my daughters continued to 'hog' it for hours on end!

- **Provide them with a separate phone line or mobile phone** – this will help you (and hopefully them!) keep a track of the hours they will inevitably spend ringing people they are just about to meet. But, of course, before giving them their phone, be clear about the financial limitations. The new pre-paid tariffs on mobiles now make separate phones a much easier and more affordable option. (They *must* have been invented by the parent of a teenager!)

- **Don't 'punish' their secrecy or solitude by giving them put-downs or hurting their feelings** – most parents feel a little 'put out' when their teenagers start to isolate themselves in their bedrooms more or become much more secretive about their activities. (Even though they may have been longing for more 'space' from them for many years!) Try to resist, even in jest, saying things like:

'I thought we'd never see you tonight.'
'Oh, so you are at home, are you?!'
'This place is becoming more and more like a hotel by the minute.'
'Why don't you want to watch the match with me anymore – it's not the same without you.'
'Hi, stranger!'

However tempting (or commonplace) it is to make such remarks, when you do, you can push them further away. In the short-term you may 'force' them to stay with you just to keep the peace or their pocket money. But in the long-term, their resentment may encourage them to stay more distant.

So, the moment you feel sidelined, remind yourself of the positive aspects of their separating themselves more from you. You will have more time to yourself, they will become more confident, and the chances are that you will eventually become even closer once they have become fully-fledged independent adults.

- **Gently challenge the embarrassment barrier, but don't crash through it** – approach sensitive subjects with care and watch out for signs of awkwardness. These may not come straightforwardly (as in red faces and giggles) but may be more indirect, such as changing the subject or always being in a hurry when particular topics come up. Remember that teenagers are often easily embarrassed because they are so self-conscious and often feel ill-at-ease, confused and out-of-control. You may be very comfortable, for example, when talking about sexual or intimate health matters with them but they may not be. (Even if they could do so happily at an earlier age.)

  Your aim should be to make conversation on *any* topic permissible but not compulsory. A gentle challenge might take the form of:
  'I know you find it difficult to talk to me about this, but nevertheless, I think it may help. You could call the shots by just telling me when we are getting onto tricky ground and you don't want to talk anymore.'

■ **Give them permission to confide in someone else** – make it clear that you would understand if they wanted to discuss some matters with someone other than you. If, for example, you guess they are having a problem or have a dilemma but they are reluctant to talk about it, you could say something like this:
'I don't want to pry but I am concerned that you may be worried about ... I can understand that you may not want to talk it over with me/us, even though I'd love to help if I can. I remember there were many things that I didn't want to discuss with my parents. But it may help to talk to someone – perhaps your friend ___ would understand. Or there is Uncle Bill – I know he knows a lot about that kind of problem and you could trust him absolutely. Or there is always the ___ organization – they give confidential advice. Their number is on this leaflet.'

Alternatively, you could 'drop the hint' that it would be okay to consult an agony aunt or uncle. You could do this by making positive comments about the letters page in the magazines or giving them one of Judy Blume's great books (for example, *Letters to Judy: What Kids Wish They Could Tell You*).

'Young people are likely to discuss issues to do with school and career with their parents, but topics relating to sex and social relationships are far more likely to be discussed with peers.'

John C. Coleman and Leo B. Hendry

■ **Encourage them to write a private diary** – or at least have a book in a lockable drawer where they can scribble down their thoughts and feelings. If they like reading, you could give them a copy of a book in diary form such as *Diary of a Young Girl* by Anne Frank or *The Secret Diary of Adrian Mole Aged 13¾* by Sue Townsend. This will indirectly give them permission to 'sound off' as much as they like about you or anyone else and explore 'silly' ideas and 'weird' feelings.

Alternatively, they might prefer to write their private thoughts down in a more creative way. Teenagers are often drawn towards poetry, song writing or even novels. Novels such as *Catcher in the Rye* by J. D. Salinger and songs by singers such as John Lennon might motivate them. If they don't like writing, suggest they keep a diary on tape. One of my own daughters often used drawings to explore her feelings and dilemmas, and she kept many of these to herself. Those that did get seen she often, quite rightly, refused to 'explain'.

Extracts from *Diary of a Young Girl:*

'12 June 1942
I hope I will be able to confide everything to you, as I have never been able to confide in anyone, and I hope you will be a great source of comfort and support.'

'3 Oct 1942
Daddy is grumbling again and threatening to take away my diary. Oh horror of horrors! From now on I am going to hide it.'

Anne Frank

- **Give them appropriate books or pamphlets** – particularly on subjects you think they may be hesitant to discuss with you, for example, drugs, sex, different religions, relationship problems, assertiveness or bullying. After reading them, they may well feel more able to open up to you, but even if they don't, at least your anxiety will be lessened knowing that they have had some important information or advice. You should also find yourself less tempted to ask the kind of prying questions that clam them up even more.

- **Expect, and accept, the occasional need to lie** – but don't condone or encourage the practise! You would have had to have been an extraordinary teenager if you never lied to your own parents. Most teen lies are not malicious or evil. They are often used as an apparently easy way of protecting their privacy or covering up their embarrassment or inadequacies.

You are more likely to successfully curb their lying by tackling the underlying causes rather than condemning them as liars. If you suspect a lie you could say something like:

'I don't know whether you're telling the truth or not. But if you aren't, I want you to know that I would much rather you told me straight that you didn't want to tell me where you have been. I might not like not knowing what you are doing because I'm such a worrier, but I'd prefer to live with that problem than have you start not being honest with me.'

'My gut feeling is telling me that I'm not quite getting the true picture here. If you really did forget to do it, I'd rather you said so – even if I blow my top at you, that wouldn't be the end of the world. You've got a right to make mistakes after all and I have been known to forget the odd thing or two as you well know!'

Of course their immediate response will probably be defensive. But you will have made your point without a head-on attack on their self-esteem. You can only trust that their need to lie will eventually pass as they begin to feel more secure in themselves. (You are actually quite powerless to do much else!)

- **Be a good role model** – protect your own privacy and make sure that you have some solitude yourself. This may be hard to do as the egocentricity of teenagers often renders them notoriously disrespectful of others' need for privacy or space away from them. Standing up for your right to keep aspects of your relationship with your partner *your* private business should indicate that you will respect this right for them too. Insisting on having time to yourself will similarly show them that you appreciate the benefits of solitude, especially during times of increased pressure.

  And finally, **say yes to a lock on their door should they ask for one!**

Rule 18:
Don't be Afraid to 'Spoil' Them
with the Extras They Need

'I remember once when I was feeling mega-stressed just before my GCSE's and was convinced I would fail, mum took me away for the weekend horse riding – on my own. My sister kicked up a fuss 'cos she wanted to come as well, but mum said I needed to go on my own. Most parents would have given that kind of treat to a child if they had done well. But mum knew that I needed a bit of extra spoiling before my exams.'

Lorraine, a confident 25-year-old lab technician

On this point I know that I am speaking out on very controversial territory. Perhaps many of you will disagree with this rule. I understand that some parents feel very strongly that a) all children should be given equal opportunities and b) that any form of spoiling is wrong. I just hope that if you feel similarly, you will continue reading this section and give it some thought. If after doing so, you still disagree but accept the 20 other rules, I certainly won't complain!

Children who lack confidence are undoubtedly disadvantaged children. Their emotional deprivation can be even more limiting than many more obvious signs of deprivation. According to my value system, this means that they, along with all other disadvantaged children, can and ought to be given a little 'spoiling'. By this I mean that they deserve a better-than-average supply of anything which might help balance out the odds against them. The extras could take many forms ranging from more one-to-one time to a state-of-the-art computer. Perhaps these examples will illustrate more clearly what I mean.

Sean was making good progress in French until he reached the age of 14. His marks then began to plummet. His parents spoke to his teacher who said that it was his confidence that was now holding him back. He wouldn't speak up in class. It was frustrating for her because she knew he had the potential. Sean's parents decided to pay for him to have conversation classes with a French student living locally.

This was not as easy to do as it sounds. Sean's parents had to take some 'flack' from their two other children and their grandparents, who accused them of favouritism. None of their other children had had any private tuition. But they still stood firm by their decision and explained why they had made it.

The following year Sean's marks were at the level they should have been and he was participating in class role-plays with some enthusiasm.

Emily had been a bit of a 'loner' all her life. She was very close to her mother who had been a single parent for the last 10 years. By the age of 15 most of her girlfriends had paired up with boys and she found herself more often than not on her own at the weekends. If she was invited out, she would quickly make up an excuse about why she couldn't go. She was rapidly losing confidence and also interest in her appearance.

Emily's mother decided to 'spoil' her by sending her on a drama activity holiday. (In her last school Emily had taken a leading role in most productions but she hadn't acted for several years, saying she hadn't the time to do so now.) Before Emily went her mother also arranged for her to have a total makeover with an image consultant and gave her an allowance to buy a number of new outfits.

On her return, Emily joined the local amateur operatic society. In order to give her more time to attend rehearsal, Emily's mother had to constantly make 'compromises' over the household chore rota. Her worries about spoiling her daughter disappeared the night she attended her first performance in a leading role and saw her happily run off to join the cast for their after-show party.

Emily is now at university and having a full social life. She has recently applied to become a volunteer with a third world charity. She has grown up to become a confident and socially responsible, caring adult – in spite of the traumas in her earlier life and her subsequent spoiling!

Dan is the youngest child of a large family. He was often jokingly described as an 'afterthought' because he arrived seven years after the last of his four brothers. Times had been financially hard for many years for his parents, but they felt proud and pleased that their four eldest boys had done very well in spite of the economic hardship. Dan was less successful in his schoolwork than the others but seemed 'happy enough'.

By the time Dan reached the age of 16 his parents had, at last, enough money to be able to think about a holiday abroad for themselves. Dan said he didn't want to go, so it was agreed he would go and stay with his friend. His parents were at the point of booking their holiday when they received a call from Dan's IT teacher. He explained that he was ringing because Dan had said that he didn't have a computer at home and that he didn't want to ask for one because of his parents' financial situation. He said that he had been taking a special interest in Dan because he had shown a talent for this subject and had noticed that he had grown in confidence as a result. He went on to say that he knew of a second-hand computer that was for sale and wondered if there was any chance that they could buy it for him.

Dan's parents were shocked. They had no idea that he had wanted a computer or that he appeared to lack confidence at school. In fact, they thought he wasn't particularly interested in IT (or any other school subject, for that matter). Dan, like many other teens I have known, was doing a brilliant 'cover-up job' on his lack of inner confidence. Outwardly he affected a cocky persona, but inwardly his self-esteem was very shaky. (Maybe his IT teacher had spotted the problem because he could identify with Dan or maybe he was just a sensitive man doing an excellent job!)

Once his parents knew the situation, they had no hesitation at all in postponing their holiday. They talked to Dan and explained that this was what they *wanted* to do and not what they felt they had to do. Eventually he was convinced and a new (not second-hand and out-of-date) computer was bought.

Dan has now taught his parents how to use his computer. They are thrilled as they now email the rest of the family and their friends who moved to Australia. His mother has also recently started to use it to do the bookkeeping for her husband's plumbing business. And his father is now talking about surfing the net to search for a holiday in Greece at a knockdown price!

Needless to say, Dan's confidence has been considerably boosted. Previously he had always felt on the margins of his family and inwardly felt that he had never been taken seriously. (He had always been referred to as 'the baby' or 'my kid brother'.)

With hindsight it is easy to say that his parents made the right decision. They were left with no regrets and Dan had no disabling guilt. But at the time they made their decision, I wonder how many other people might have thought that the apparently over-confident Dan was being spoiled.

Top Tips

- **Be courageous in the face of judgemental attitudes from others, including your children**. This kind of 'spoiling' often does cause raised eyebrows, even from adults who should know better! Remember that you are not being unfair if you give a needy, anxious child more attention and resources than a child who is more confident.

- **Use your intuition and values, as well as your bank balance, as your guide**. Give your teen what *you* believe you can and want to afford and what *feels right* to you. Be proud of your decision and don't feel you have to justify it in financial terms. For example: *'It will pay dividends in the long run. I know if he passes this exam, he is more likely to get a better job.'*

- **Explain to your teen (and their siblings) why you are giving them the 'extras'**. For example:
'We are giving you extra coaching because your confidence has taken such a knock since we moved. Angie is a little younger and it hasn't been so hard for her to adapt – her schoolwork hasn't suffered. But we still love you both equally and if Angie ever needs some extra help she will get it.'
or,

'I want to give John a treat to take his mind off the exams. You know he gets especially nervous. I think taking him to the match will do the trick, but I can only afford two tickets. I am very proud of you for being so understanding.'

> **Be courageous in the face of judgemental attitudes from others. Follow your intuition and values. Give your teen what *you* believe they need and what *you* can afford and *you* want to give.**

Rule 19:
Celebrate the Milestones as
well as the Achievements

> 'A joy that is shared is a joy made double.'
>
> English proverb

Once again, we have a rule that is much harder to put into practise than it first seems. Most parents know the theory. They know that it is important to encourage each small step in their children's development. Listening to conversations at the junior school gate or on parents' evenings, it is not uncommon to overhear comments such as:

'I don't care if she is bottom of the class, as long as she is happy.'
'All I need to know is that he has done his best.'
'Don't worry, darling! We can't all be good at everything.'

But by the time their children reach senior school their attitude often changes. Achieving end-goals becomes a seriously competitive business. Final results, rather than valiant efforts, are now all-important. The milestone achievements en route are barely noticed. It is not these that will determine children's futures. The 'bottom line' is that it is only top grades and first prizes that can guarantee future security and happiness.

Is it any wonder that teenagers feel under so much pressure? Or that the confidence of those who cannot reach standards of excellence plummets?

The world of leading-edge business is just beginning to wake-up to the folly of this thinking. Some influential leaders in the field are now questioning what effect the pursuit of 'end-results at all costs' has. Many have found out through personal experience that in the long run, it doesn't pay. They have seen their most talented staff lose their confidence, become demotivated and crack from stress. Leaders are now being urged by their gurus to value and reward effort at every step along the production line. Posters with the slogan 'Success is a journey, not a destination' now commonly adorn office walls.

Unfortunately, these posters and their message have yet to reach the average school classroom! The schools in my country are more likely to have their eyes firmly fixed on final results. It is hard to blame them. These are what the teachers are now judged by. These are what can make or break a school financially. What this means in terms of your teenager's confidence, is that you cannot rely on their school to reward their milestone achievements. You must do it and encourage them to do it for themselves. It won't be easy. You will probably meet much resistance. You may need to remind them that long-lasting inner confidence can only be built small step by small step. And the completion of each of these needs to be appreciated just as much as the more dramatic leaps forward. (After all, luck more often than not deserves much of the credit for major successes.)

> 'Everything I did was applauded – all the trivial milestones of child-hood were celebrated.'
>
> Professor Susan Greenfield, first female director of Royal Institute of Great Britain

Top Tips

- **Don't promise big rewards for big achievements** – very often parents mistakenly think they are helping their children by telling them they will give them a large sum of money, a special holiday, or a much wanted new gadget *if* they achieve good results. This kind of 'bribery' may sometimes work in the short-term, but as we discussed in Rule 7, in the long-term what they need is the ability to motivate themselves without being dependent on 'carrots' from others. Once a goal has been achieved you can, of course, reward to your heart's content. But, ironically that is the time when their confidence least needs that kind of help. It is at earlier times when their confidence is at its most shaky that your positive input is most needed.

- **Keep the celebrations appropriate to the achievement *or* the effort** – if you 'go over the top' with rewards, their resistance to accepting the 'compliment' will understandably be stronger. Even if they enjoy whatever you have given them, if they don't feel their effort has deserved such a reward, it will do nothing for their self-esteem.

- **Don't go in for public broadcasts** – otherwise they may become embarrassed and over-anxious. Teenagers are always looking over their shoulders at their peer's progress and are always convinced that others are doing better. They also tend to play down their own achievements to their friends. You may not like this competitive cultural habit, but you're unlikely to beat it. So rather than fight it, respect it by keeping your celebrations within the family.

- **Surprise them** – with an unexpected treat or presents. They would have to be a very unusual teenager to refuse their favourite desert or return a wanted gift.

- **Be prepared to wait (sometimes forever!) for their thanks** – the fact that they may not express much gratitude or appreciation for this kind of support does not mean that the 'magic' isn't working. They may not realize how important it was until several years later. Most will give you thanks when they do. But for some, they may not reach this insight until it is too late. I have heard quite a number of people tell me that their deceased parents' early encouragement was vital to their progress and express regret at not being appreciative enough at the time.

- **Celebrate your own small achievements** – and invite them to join in. Demonstrate how the journey can be as much fun as reaching the destination!

> Show them how the journey to success can be as much fun as reaching the destination!

Rule 20:
Find, and Keep Alive, a New Dream for You

> 'If you have built castles in the air, your work need not be lost; that is where they should be. Now put the foundations under them.'
>
> Henry David Thoreau

Don't wait for your teen to leave home before planning what you have always wanted to do. At the very least, put the wheels of your dream machine in motion and make sure that its engine has a regular service!

The empty nest syndrome is not just a cliché, it's a real threat to all committed and caring parents. None of us should think we are immune to its potential threat to our own happiness or the ability of our children to fly freely and happily from our nest.

At this moment in time, you may find it difficult to believe that you could be struck down with feelings of apathy and sadness as you wave goodbye to the responsibilities of parenting. You probably already fantasize about the peace and freedom this will bring. (Most parents do!) But, unless you are already well-engaged in pursuing a new dream for you, you may find this time depressing rather than uplifting. You may no longer even want to pursue a dream, let alone have the energy to do so.

This rule is even more important to keep in mind if currently you are not satisfied or content with your life. This is because parents in this state often depend too heavily on the presence of their teen to keep their spirit alive. This kind of dependency can be so restricting for children. I can't tell you how many stories I have heard from timid adults who told me that they found it difficult to leave home because they felt worried or guilty about either one or both of their parents. In the following examples, it seems that the family's apron strings were made of steel!

> 'I feel so sorry for her ... she never had the education I had. She's been a housewife all her life. She'd had the odd part-time job, but she could have been so much more. She always said she was looking forward to the day

> *we all left home but when I did, she was on the phone almost every night ... I don't mind, we are very close ... Yes, it probably has held me back, but now she's getting elderly and has so few friends.'*

> *'He has had such a hard life – working all hours at a job he hated, just for us. Then they made him redundant and he became so depressed. My mum often said that she didn't know how they'd manage if I wasn't around.'*

> *'I know they stayed together just for us. I became a sort of bridge between them. The only time they talked to each other was when I was around.'*

These next examples illustrate how sometimes these kinds of emotional ties are only visible when a therapist like me starts digging well below the surface.

> **John** recounted how his mother professed to be delighted that he had applied to do voluntary work in Africa during his gap year. But he also knew that a) she had always regretted not doing the same when she was 18 and b) that now she was swallowing daily doses of Prozac to keep herself cheerful. He worried that she wouldn't be able to cope when he was out of phone contact.

> **Adam** told me that he had heard his parents telling his teacher that they hoped he would go to university somewhere far from home. They thought that would be such a confidence-building experience for him. But whenever he went on a school trip, instead of going away for a holiday of their own, they insisted on staying at home to be there *'in case anything went wrong and you need to get in touch or come home.'*

> **Jenny** knew that her mother had a brilliant singing voice and had always dreamed of being a member of a choir. When she tried to encourage her to go for singing lessons, she refused saying: *'Don't you worry about me. There'll be plenty of time for all that sort of thing when you leave home. I want to enjoy being with you while you're here. I see little enough of you now as it is.'*

But keeping your dreams alive can also be helpful to your children in the present. Adults who are looking forward excitedly to their future are much more inspiring to be with and usually much more supportive of teenage adventures than those who dread the empty nest.

Many teens do of course manage to leave home in spite of leaving behind parents who are unhappy and unfulfilled. But their confidence may suffer as a result. Because they cannot wait to get away from the depressing and boring atmosphere, they may leave home too early for their own good. As a result, they can take risks for which they are ill-equipped and then suffer endless demotivating knock-backs and failures.

Others may have to 'harden their hearts' in order to leave their unhappy parents. Doing this is never good for self-esteem and almost always makes it harder for them to thrive in other intimate relationships.

> 'Just before she died my mother said "I wish I had your life". It was painful to hear her say that. I didn't want her to want my life. I wanted her to have enjoyed her own.'
>
> Margaret Forster

Top tips

- **Never lose sight of what you have placed on your back burner** – keep an eye on the dreams and projects you have shelved while you are parenting. If, for example, one of your dreams is to visit a certain far-off country, you could keep it alive by reading books and watching films about it. You could also, perhaps, find a way of meeting people who have already visited it or lived there. Maybe you could even learn to dance their dances or speak their language. One of my own dreams is to visit Argentina. I have been learning the Tango and Spanish for several years and as my nest is now well and truly empty, I am about to book my ticket!

- **Critically reappraise your dreams every so often** – I can't think of any experiences which have changed me and my aspirations more than having children! Parenting developed new sides of my character and my daughters' interests opened up worlds I would never have even thought to look into. My dreams for my own future subsequently changed. But, being a professional in this personal development business, I made sure that I didn't abandon one dream without replacing it with another!

- **Start getting into action well before they leave** – my job not only helped to place a high value on having life-dreams, it also gave me plenty of forewarning about empty nest problems. I knew that even though I currently had a full and happy life, I would still feel pain when my daughters no longer needed to be near to me. (I guessed they would want to travel the world.) I had counselled many people through this life-stage, so I was fortunate to be able to learn from their mistakes. The biggest lesson I learned was how important it is to be actively involved in pursuing a dream while they are in their later teenage years. Doing this helps divert your attention from their increasing absence and gives them an inspiring and lively role model to come home to when the fancy takes them!

> 'My parents sacrificed so much for us – they've only just started taking holidays abroad. They say they don't begrudge anything but I always felt guilty if I was out having a good time. They seem to have wasted the best years of their life. Dad's now got a heart condition so it's too late for him to go climbing the Himalayas. That's been a dream of his for as long as I can remember.'
>
> a 35-year-old parent being counselled for depression

Rule 21:
Nail the Door Ajar – Forever!

> ' ... the first thing I did when I was told they were axing my last show was to ring home. I'm lucky, my parents are really cool – I've always known that they'd be there for me whenever the going gets tough. I go home often – a weekend there is great for de-stressing ... It's nothing to do with "home cooking" – in fact, mum's a pretty dreadful cook – it's just that there I can be completely myself and I don't feel I'm being judged or on show. Just what I need when my confidence has had a hammering – and in this business that happens pretty frequently, I can assure you.'
>
> Mike, a 34-year-old radio presenter

So yes, we need to make it as easy as possible for our teenagers to leave the nest. But equally, it is just as important to make it just as easy for them to return whenever they may need to do so. This, you'll be pleased to learn, is the final delicate balancing act that, as a parent of a teen, you may have to perform!

Some children have no problem barging through their parents' door at any time of the day or night throughout their whole life. But those with shaky confidence almost certainly will be reticent to do so. The irony, of course, is that it is these children who need the door to stay ajar forever the most.

It's not good enough to assume that because our children know that they are deeply loved, they will feel free to return whenever they have a problem or need a dose of love and security. Some children seem to need this message spelt out in flashing neon lighting straight in front of their noses! (If you are not sure whether your child is one of these, assume they are!)

I have recently spoken to a number of youth counsellors about this problem. They say that they spend many hours persuading young people to re-establish contact with their parents. They are not talking about forcing them back into the arms of abusive or self-centred fathers and mothers. They are talking about persuading them to return to parents who would give up virtually anything in their world to ensure that their children were happy and secure.

The teenagers are not frightened to go home because they will be hit or even verbally slapped. Some of the most common reasons for their reluctance to return are that they believe that one or both of their parents:

- will be disappointed (perhaps they have failed an exam or decided they have chosen the wrong course and feel disappointed in themselves)
- are too busy (perhaps they need time to talk NOW and think their parents have immovable commitments)
- are too stressed by their own problems (perhaps they know their parents have more than their fair share of personal or work problems)
- are too poor (perhaps they have misperceived their parents' thrift as dire poverty)
- do not deserve to have a failure for a child (perhaps they feel indebted to their parents for being so generous and supportive for so long)

How would you feel if you thought that your child would not turn to you in times of difficulty for one of these reasons?

You would probably feel the same as their parents did – horrified! I guess you might also feel desperately sad and possibly a little guilty. Your mind would probably become besieged with 'if onlys'.

No aspect of parenting behaviour or effort ever comes with a guarantee. There will always be children who will misperceive good intentions and misinterpret clear messages. But you may be able to avoid some problems by doing the following:

Top Tips
- **Ensure that they always know your whereabouts or have your contact numbers** – even if they don't want to reciprocate or say they don't need them (you can say it is for *your* peace of mind, not theirs – that would only be half a white lie!)

- **Say clearly that their needs are at the top of your priority list** – and add that this will continue for as long as you or they live.

- **Put this message in writing from time to time** – hopefully they won't always believe what they see written in black and white, but a sincere reinforcement on a card from you is likely to make this message stick more firmly.

- **Tell them you will always love them 'unconditionally'** – but make sure they know what you mean. They need to know that it means you will not stop loving them, even if they behave in ways that sometimes disappoint or puzzle you.

- **Warn them that they may feel reluctant to come back** – whilst in the security of your home they may not be able to imagine they could ever hesitate. Say you will understand if they do feel embarrassed or fearful or guilty and share times when you have felt similarly.

- **Tell them that you are confident that any 'drop-back' visits will be temporary** – it may help them to know that you believe that they have the capability to stand on their own two feet again. After a failure, we often doubt our capacity to do so.

- **Make it clear that you do not expect them to abuse your 'ever-open' door** – hopefully you will know how to get this message across in an unthreatening way! In your own words, you could, for example, say:

  'I know you love us and would never just use us.'

  'If it doesn't work out, you know there is always a bed here. I know you'll always pay your way if you can, so don't worry if you happen to be broke at the time.'

  or using a humorous tone:

  'I want you to know that our home, wherever it is, will always be your home if you need it to be. But I trust that if you do decide to drop in, you'll give us good warning whenever you can!'

  'If you can force yourself to stomach the house rules once again, you know the key of the door is yours forever!'

part two

Putting the Golden Rules into Practice

The Angst Tests

Now it is exam time for you!

Here is a chance to see how you might apply the Golden Rules and any other parenting theory or knowledge you have. I will be presenting you with five real-life problem situations and asking you to step into the shoes of an agony aunt or uncle to come up with some helpful advice. Although the characters in our imaginary stories do not exist in reality, the problems and issues they raise most certainly do. They are typical of those which confront parents of teenagers on a regular basis.

I have divided the chapter into two sections. It is important that you read the first section before the second one (otherwise you will have to mark yourself down for cheating!) In the first section, you will find:

- a short background summary of the family situation
- a letter from a parent outlining the current problem
- questions to ask yourself or discuss with your co-parent and/or family and friends. Some of you may even feel you might like to discuss some of the problems with your own teenager (if they are mature and interested enough to do so). I understand that teenagers avidly read agony columns but, of course, they usually see letters from their peers rather than the parents.

In the second section, you will find some of my own thoughts on the problem. I have also given some ideas on what the parent could do and which of the Golden Rules might be helpful.

I hope these little 'tests' will be interesting to do. They may give you a clearer idea of how confident you would feel if you happened to be faced with similar issues. I hope they will also stimulate some challenging debate within your family or social circles.

The Problems

'You always take her side'

Family background

Gillian is a single parent. She and her husband were amicably divorced five years ago. Gillian works part-time as a nurse. She has not had a serious relationship since her divorce and is not currently interested in one. She says her social life with a group of colleagues is *'Enough for the moment. I have no time or energy for anything else!'*

Their children (John, aged 15, and Anna, aged 12) stay with their father every other weekend. He remarried 3 years ago and now lives 40 miles away. He has a new baby girl who is twelve months old. John gets on well with his father, who shares many of his leisure interests such as football and classic cars. John doesn't talk much to Gillian about his weekends and she prides herself on not probing him about them. Anna, on the other hand, chatters happily about how she has helped with the baby and has a large picture of her new sister in her bedroom.

Letter from Gillian

'I had a terrible scene with my son, John, yesterday. He started accusing me again of favouring his sister, Anna, who is a couple of years younger. I got upset and started shouting back at him. I bend over backwards to be fair and I had just had enough.

I felt very bad afterwards and I did apologize, but by then he was locked in his shell again and wouldn't talk. I know it is hard for him because Anna is doing much better at school than he did and is very attractive – she is always the one that other people tend to look at first. The house is now often full of her friends. I think John may feel a bit excluded because when he and Anna were young they used to be together most of the time.

I know John lacks confidence – he always has. His teachers say he doesn't speak up enough in class and that's one of the reasons he is lagging behind. It's becoming more important than ever now as he will soon be doing his GCSE orals in French and German. I just don't know how he is going to cope.

I know his temper tantrums and jealousy are partly due to his worry about these exams, but I can't just stand by, especially when he starts having an unfair go at Anna. She's usually done nothing wrong – last Tuesday she just came down to breakfast in a new tee-shirt and he made some snide remark about it. She snapped back at him and walked off to school without having any breakfast. Prompted by me, he usually apologizes to her when he realizes he has hurt her, but then he can do it again the next day.

I know you're supposed to let them fight it out themselves at their age, but it is always John who seems to start the scenes and I can't help feeling that Anna is losing out.

I'm sure I do love them both absolutely equally and have never taken sides before, but John just seems to know how to provoke me.

I have talked it over with my ex-husband. His attitude is that it's just a phase and that I should just lighten up about it. He thinks John's a bit shy, but doesn't think he has a big problem with confidence.'

Questions to ask yourself

- Is John's behaviour 'normal' or 'abnormal' for his age?
- Is it a good idea for Gillian to 'bend over backwards' to be fair?
- Which aspects of the family situation could have a bearing on the problem?
- What is Gillian doing well as a parent?
- What could Gillian do to help herself stay in control of her own feelings?
- When talking to John after a 'crisis', what should Gillian try to avoid doing or saying?
- What kinds of phrases or words might be helpful for Gillian to use?

■ What else could Gillian do or do differently that might help the situation?

Once you have given these questions some thought, turn to page 167 for some of my own ideas on what Gillian could do to help John.

'She thinks she's fat and ugly'

Family background

Karen, aged 14, is the oldest of five children. Her father, Eddie, is a long-distance lorry driver, so he is often away from home. Her mother, Pat, has been a full-time housewife most of Karen's life, but recently has taken on a part-time job in a supermarket. Karen looks after the house and her brothers and sister if her father is away and her mother is out working. Everyone who meets the family comments on how like her mother Karen looks and sounds.

Pat and Eddie's marriage is strong in spite of their times apart, and Karen's three brothers and sister appear to be thriving and developing normally. Their lifestyle is modest, but there are no serious financial worries.

Letter from Pat

'I've been talking to a friend at work who thinks my daughter, Karen, could be getting anorexic – I can hardly get her to eat anything now. When I tell her she looks as thin as a rake and she must eat, she says she's not hungry. She thinks she's fat and ugly.

She's always been such a good girl and never been any trouble. And she's still such a great help to me with the others. They all love her to bits – and so do I. I tell her over and over again that she is special and that I don't know what I'd do without her. But lately I don't seem to be able to get near her – she pushes me away if I try to cuddle her.

I took her to town last Saturday to buy her a dress to wear over Christmas but we came home with nothing again. She said nothing fitted her, although everyone in the shops told her she looked great. She's not ugly at all – she's got big brown eyes and beautiful hair with a natural curl. Her skin is lovely – much better than most of her friends. She's a bit on the short side, like me.

Eddie says I'm too soft with her at mealtimes. When he's home, he makes her sit down till she's finished, but I am thinking now, after what my friend was saying, that she may secretly be making herself sick afterwards. She's always the first to leave the table and goes upstairs to do her homework. She says she goes up so she can get some peace to study in before Jane (her younger sister) comes up and starts playing her music. I've asked her directly if she ever makes herself sick and she just said: "Don't be silly mum, stop fussing. Do you think I would?"

Eddie agrees I'm fussing – he thinks she looks fine – but he doesn't know her like I do (he's closer to the boys because they talk football day and night together!) He says it's good she's not growing up too quickly and that it's her friends who are wrong – he says they look tarty in their make-up and tight tops.

She works very hard at her schoolwork and always gets good reports. We were very proud of her last year – she was fifth in her whole year. Her teacher said she'll easily get into university to do a science degree if she continues to work as hard as she does. She is a bit shy, but she does have a group of mates who she gets on well with. They all seem much more confident and older than she does – maybe it's because they wear make-up and a few of them already have boyfriends.

I want her to go out more and have fun – she's a bit too serious. But she says she's fine as she is. I've told her she doesn't have to baby-sit the others anymore – they can stay at my neighbours until I get home from work. (I'm home by 8 pm.)

Should I make her go to the doctors? She says it's my imagination and that she hasn't lost weight, she's putting it on. I'm sure she has, though it's difficult to tell because she's always in jeans and baggy tee-shirts. But she could be right – I am a bit of a worrier.'

Questions to ask yourself

■ Does it sound as though Pat has good reason to worry as much as she is? Is it likely that Karen has a serious eating disorder, or do you think that her friend (perhaps in response to media 'hype') might have raised her anxiety unnecessarily?

■ Does it sound as though her husband is right and Pat is being too soft with Karen over the eating issue? Could she be letting Karen slip into a habit of eating less than she needs?

■ Is lack of confidence one of the reasons behind eating disorders?

■ What comments would you make about Karen's relationship with her parents? Do you think that either relationship could have a bearing on the situation?

■ Are there any clues in the story which point to possible problems with confidence?

■ Should Pat take her daughter to the doctor now or should she wait until she has more 'hard evidence' of a problem? (What would the 'hard evidence' be that she might be looking for?)

■ What can Pat do or stop doing that might help Karen to feel good about herself and her body?

Turn to page 171 for the answers to these questions and to find out which of the Golden Rules might help Pat with her problem.

'He's C-stream in everything and he knows it'

Family background

Sean is almost 18 years old and is the only son of Brian and Jill, who are both in senior positions in international banking. Brian worked his way to the top with no higher education. He met Jill en route. She has an MBA and is more academically-orientated than he is. Both are also committed voluntary workers and sit on various charitable committees.

Sean was adopted when both Brian and Jill were in their late thirties. They are highly committed parents even though much of Sean's day-care in earlier years was left to a series of nannies and au pairs.

Approximately six years ago, Brian and Jill sought help for their marriage. The couple were separated for a few months after it was revealed that Brian had been having an affair. Their decision to live together again was very much influenced by their sense of joint responsibility to parenting Sean.

Letter from Brian

'You'll be pleased to hear that Jill and I seem to have sorted things out and we've been getting on much better during the last two or three years. We're both still working too much and still making resolutions to take it easier – but that's no surprise to you, I'm sure!

We would now really appreciate your advice on how to help our son, Sean. We are very concerned that he may have a serious self-esteem problem. He was no problem at all until he failed 50% of his GCSE's. He wanted then to leave school immediately. (He was 16 years old.) We agreed, on the understanding that he attended a crammer college in the summer and retook his GCSE's. He scraped a pass in another two subjects. Since then, however, he has done virtually nothing. He spends most of the day watching TV and videos at home. In the evenings he's out with his friends and more often than not, he comes back having drunk far too much. From time-to-time he gets a labouring job to earn some money, but he's not really cut out for that kind of physical heavy work and he quickly gets bored.

He doesn't know what he wants to do. I've offered to pay for him to see a private psychologist specializing in career advice, but he won't go. He's says he'd rather have the same money for a round-the-world ticket. He wants to go travelling for six months to a year. He says that would give him a chance to think, and then he promises to get a job on his return.

As you know we have never pushed him further than he wanted to go. We have always known his academic limitations and we just want him to be happy in whatever he decides he wants to do. When he is on form he has a great personality and could go far just with that. He's very popular with his group of friends. In the past he's had many girlfriends, but he says he's not interested in them at the moment. He's never had any hobbies and since leaving school he hasn't even played football.

I think the crux of the problem is that he is C-stream and he knows it. He is also convinced that he'll never get a decent job because all employers are demanding degrees now.

How can we help him to feel better about himself and more positive about his future? He doesn't seem to take any reassurances from us. I am worried that to let him go travelling now would be avoiding the real problem. I think he should show some motivation to do something first. I've suggested a three-month IT course that I know is starting soon. I've said if he sticks to that, I'll be more convinced that he can look after himself while he is away. After all, he'll have to stick it out at jobs en route if he's going for that long.

Jill thinks we should let him go now because he'll just do the minimum on the IT course, as he did at the crammer college. She also thinks a touch of the hard life fending for himself is what will help him most at the moment.'

Questions to ask yourself

■ What emotions might you guess that Brian is feeling which could be influencing his handling of this situation?

■ Assuming Sean's self-esteem is at a low ebb, are there any historical factors which *could* have contributed to this problem? If so, do you think they need to be unearthed before Sean can make much more progress? What might be an argument against doing this?

■ With hindsight, do you think it was a good idea for his parents to insist that Sean went to the crammer college?

■ What would be the pros and cons of giving Sean the money to go travelling now?

■ What might be some alternative actions which Brian and Jill could take to help their son if they decide not to give him money to go travelling?

■ Reading between the lines, do you think that Brian and Jill (and indirectly Sean) might benefit from working on their own lives, or relationship, or personalities?

Turn to page 174 for the answers to these questions and some of my own thoughts on how Brian and Jill can help Sean.

'He's too easily led'

Family Background

David, aged 13, is the youngest son of Carol and Roger. They have two other sons Billy, aged 17, and Paul, aged 19. They are essentially a happy and close family. They have all led fairly conventional and uneventful lives. A close neighbour recently described them as 'quiet, extremely kind and a joy to have as neighbours. The boys are always so polite and well-behaved.'

Roger has his own small accountancy practise and Carol is a teacher. Billy has just been offered a place at university to do engineering and Paul is currently doing a degree in economics at a university a couple of hundred miles away from home. Both have steady relationships with girlfriends whom their parents know and like.

Letter from Roger

'I'm sorry to bother you with our problem – I'm sure you have much more serious ones to deal with. We are probably worrying about nothing, but it would be good to get your advice. We are a bit worried about our youngest son, David. For the last few months, he seems to be going around with a particular group of boys whom we have never met. They don't go to his school. He met them at the ice rink where he goes every Saturday morning. (He's a good skater and has been winning medals in the sport for several years.)

He used to be quite a quiet lad, but recently he has started to be cheeky, especially when we ask him to help around the house. I lost my cool with him last weekend when he was downright rude to his mother. She had only asked him if he wanted another helping of pie. He replied, "Do you want me to get as fat as you?" He said he was only joking, but I know he wasn't.

When he is at home, he now spends most of his time in his bedroom playing his music. Billy is always getting mad at him because he says he can't concentrate on his work. He has exams soon. But then they have never really got on. He was always much closer to Paul.

My partner mentioned that he saw David a few Saturdays ago coming out of a pub with a group of older lads at lunchtime. David emphatically denies that it was him and says he was still at the ice rink. I believe him, but my wife believes my partner's story. She thought one of David's shirts smelt of smoke last week. She also has had to twice replace his bus fare recently as he claims he has had it stolen. (It's true the school has had a stealing problem recently.)

David's school reports are still very good, although a few of the teachers say that he doesn't speak up enough in class. He is probably just going through a normal adolescent phase, but we are just worried that he may get himself into a mess — he's never been as confident as the other two and is easily led.'

Questions to ask yourself
- Does it sound as though Roger is 'worrying about nothing'? Are he and his wife, Carol, being over-hasty in rushing for advice on a fairly 'normal' adolescent problem?
- How should Carol have dealt with David's rudeness? What could she have said or done in reaction?
- Should Roger talk to the school about the suspected stealing in spite of David's insistence that it wasn't him?
- What aspects of this story would make you think that David might be lacking in confidence?
- Are there any clues that Roger and Carol's relationship might be 'in need of attention' in spite of their neighbour's assessment?
- Is there anything else about the family situation which might be significant?

Turn to page 178 for some of my own ideas on what Roger and Carol can do to help David.

'She won't talk about losing her father'

Family background

Isabel's husband was killed in a car crash two months ago. Isabel is currently attending counselling sessions, and has just returned to her work as a librarian.

Isabel has two children. Her son, Bob, aged 25, now works in New York. And her 17-year-old daughter, Tina, is at the beginning of her last year at school. Tina is an above-average grade student and wants to read law at university, with a view to becoming a solicitor. Her father was a successful barrister. The family have always been very close and supportive of each other.

Tina has no boyfriend at the moment, though her ex is still a friend and has been very supportive to her. She has one close friend with whom she spends almost all her leisure time.

Letter from Isabel

'I'm worried about my daughter, Tina. I don't know how to help her.

Immediately after my husband died she was wonderful – I was in such a state, I didn't know what I was doing. She took care of all the practical arrangements – she virtually arranged the funeral by herself. I was so surprised because she was so much stronger than I thought she would ever be. She's always been on the shy side but she coped brilliantly with all the visitors, etc. I was useless.

Now I am feeling stronger I can face the world a bit again and I want to help her. But she is distancing herself from me. She won't talk about my husband or the accident – she says she can't cope with it; she has to get down to her work. She gets into real states about her homework – she keeps saying she has forgotten everything and is sure that she will fail. (She has set her heart on going to university next year and won't even consider a gap year.) Her best friend has been trying to help and rings virtually every evening, but I'm afraid she will give up on her soon. Tina always makes excuses now about why she can't go out.

I've suggested that she should also come to Cruse for grief counselling, but she says she is fine – that's not the problem; she blames herself for not having worked harder last year. I know she must be missing my husband – they were very close even though they often argued, usually about silly things.

Her brother works in the States – he came back for the funeral. He rings often but Tina won't talk to him about losing her father either. He's offered to have her to stay for a while in New York, but she says she can't afford the time. She says she might go with me in the summer.

I'm really afraid that she might be right about the exams – she could fail them because she can't concentrate for long at all. If she did, she may lose even more confidence. I've spoken to her tutor who says that she appears to be doing OK at school and thinks she will have plenty of time to catch up. He has suggested she sees the counsellor at school but she has refused.

Questions to ask yourself

- Why is it common to lose confidence after a bereavement, especially of someone close?
- Are there any special factors to take into consideration in relation to teenagers and grieving?
- Is Isabel right to be worried about the fact that her daughter won't discuss the accident or talk about her father?
- From the few details you know about Tina's relationship with her father, which aspects do you think might be significant?
- What help could Isabel and Tina reasonably expect from the school in this situation?
- What advantages and what disadvantages might there be for Tina if she were to take a gap year?
- What could Isabel say or do to help Tina when she is getting into a state about her homework? And what should she try to avoid saying or doing?
- What else could Isabel do to help her daughter?

■ Can you name any other sources of help Tina or Isabel might be able to draw on?

■ How long do you think it might be before Tina is back to her 'normal self'?

Now turn to page 181 for some of my own thoughts on Isabel's problem and how she can help Tina.

Answer Time!

'You always take her *side'*: How can Gillian help?

'7 November 1942
... Mother butted in: "Margot was reading that book; give it back to her".
Father came in, and without even knowing what was going on, saw that Margot was being wronged and lashed out at me ... it wasn't right of Father to pass judgement without even knowing what the issue was. I would have given Margot the book a lot sooner, if Father and Mother hadn't intervened.'

'12 January 1943
Margot's much nicer. She seems a lot different from what she used to be. She's not nearly as catty these days and is becoming a real friend.'

Anne Frank

Certainly a substantial degree of sibling rivalry is very normal at this age. Perhaps it might help Gillian to know that it can also be a positive learning experience. It can be an important way of learning how to handle the mixed bag of emotions that we encounter in intimate relationships, as well as learning about how to negotiate and resolve conflicts. But if sibling rivalry is not handled well, it can of course damage confidence. If John is allowed to bully or manipulate Anna whom he loves, he will undoubtedly hate himself for doing so. (I know that the fact that, as a teenager, I routinely started my confessions to the priest with 'I have bullied my brother', did little to repair my crumbling self-esteem.)

So Gillian is right to interfere when she spots John bullying his sister. This is a situation where parents should focus on fairness and help their children to do the same. John is essentially abusing his power as an older child and must be confronted with the fact that he is doing so. However, Gillian must realize the limits of her power in this situation. By 'bending over backwards' too far in order to protect Anna, she could make the situation worse. She could drive a wedge between brother and sister, which might take years (if ever) to repair. Certainly, she will only make a bad situation worse by using aggressive bullying tactics back. She needs to use assertive behaviour instead.

Additionally, Gillian needs to tackle some of the root causes that may be fuelling John's jealousy. (So, ironically, she may also have to do what may seem a bit unfair.) She should consider giving John more (and not less) attention for a while because she is probably right to think that he is lacking in confidence. But it wouldn't help the situation to offer this 'interpretation' to John himself – an 'I know what you are like' approach from parents to teens is like the proverbial red rag to a bull. Instead, she could try to help him by:

- relaxing her own 'rule' about talking to him about his weekends with his father. What she is probably frightened of is a) getting upset and jealous herself about her husband's new life and b) expressing negative feelings, either verbally or non-verbally, to John about his father (she knows John loves and needs his father).
- brushing up on her listening skills could help her to contain her own 'stuff' and help John express any ambivalent or negative feelings he might have about the new baby and losing some of his father's attention. (This must have happened, surely!) (See Rule 3.)
- resisting the temptation to play John's comparison game by saying, for example: *'Anna's younger than you'* or *'When I take your side Anna doesn't start yelling at me that I'm favouring you'*, or trying to *prove* he is wrong with facts. Statistics about how many times she took his side against Anna during the last ten years will pass him by. He is not in a logical frame of mind because his emotions and vulnerability will make it almost impossible for him to think rationally.
- watching out for the 'amateur psychologist' within herself and holding back on 'auto-pilot' remarks, such as: *'I know you don't really mean that'* or *'You're just jealous'* or *'You're too sensitive'*.

- practising her deep breathing and relaxation exercises to help her stay calm, and learning how to express herself more assertively. (See Rule 15.)
- encouraging John to share his jealousy by perhaps sharing an experience of her own. For example:
  'I know you're really pleased that Anna got into the A-stream last week, but I was wondering if you felt OK about it afterwards. I remember when Jill at work was promoted to senior manager after only two years. Although I was pleased for her, I did feel a bit jealous – it took me five years.'
- suggesting ways John can repair his dented self-esteem. Or do this indirectly, by again sharing how she (hopefully!) repaired her own. For example:
  'I had to remind myself that I'd done really well to get there in five years considering that I only got one "A" in my last year.'
  'I remember confessing these feelings to Jim and he was great – he said, well maybe you're not the world's greatest genius, but you're great fun to work with. He offered to buy me a pint to drown my sorrows. That seemed to do the trick – I felt better.'
- talking to John about the effects of bullying behaviour on the bully and the victim. Asking him to agree a ground rule about bullying behaviour and a sanction which he believes he would deserve (for example, spending the evening in his room), which might help him to stop bullying. Then, if he does bully again, Gillian should assertively and calmly confront him and firmly insist that he goes to his room. (See Rules 5 and 14.)
- spending some extra time just with John perhaps doing (or watching) an activity which he enjoys and/or is good at. (See Rule 10.)
- helping him to manage his anxiety about his exams. (See Rule 15.)
- offering to arrange for some extra coaching in his language oral work, or buying him some language tapes, or videoing TV courses for him. (See Rule 18.)
- talking again to her ex-husband to ask him if he could spend some special time alone with John. (See Rule 10.)

'Where children feel excluded, the person best suited to help them is the one they feel excluded by.'

Helen Barrett

'She thinks she's fat and ugly':
How can Pat and Eddie help?

> 'The more my mother worried and nagged me to eat, the worse it became. I'd just give in, stuff myself at mealtimes to keep the peace – then just make myself sick afterwards.'
>
> Tracey, a 21-year-old recovering bulimic

Pat is obviously a very concerned and loving mother. It sounds as though she has done a great deal already to build her daughter's inner confidence. She has provided her with love and a stable and secure home. She openly expresses how much she values her.

Research suggests that about 70% of girls of Karen's age diet, but only one in a hundred is likely to develop anorexia and four in a hundred, bulimia. So the chances are that Karen hasn't got a serious problem. But nevertheless, it won't do any harm for her parents to keep her confidence and self-esteem well boosted during her teens, as the evidence is that a lack of either can make you more vulnerable to eating disorders. Another factor that could make Karen a little more vulnerable is her seriousness. At her age, this could indicate that she is perhaps trying to overachieve. Perfectionism and competitiveness are other characteristics of young people who develop eating disorders.

So Pat is right to keep a watchful eye on her because the earlier such disorders are recognized, the better chance there is of a full recovery. But at the same time, she should try to take the 'worrier' side of her own personality in hand. Over-protective and anxious mothering is certainly not going to help Karen. It sounds as though in her quiet way Karen is asking for more 'space' from her mother (and perhaps the rest of the family). She particularly needs to be seen as different from Pat, and that is likely to be hard because the reality is that they seem similar in personality as well as looks, and are undoubtedly very close.

Through her teens, it is also important for a girl's confidence to feel 'approved of' as a woman by her father. This is why attention-seeking flirtatious behaviour with their dads is so common at this age. It sounds as though this is unlikely to happen in this family, but it is nevertheless important that Eddie conveys to Karen that he recognizes that she is becoming an attractive, mature woman (with no hint of sexual overtones from him, of course). There is a hint of a 'daddy's little girl' in the letter.

Both parents need to bear in mind that Karen has reached an age when coercive parent power can have the opposite effect to that which they might desire. Forcing Karen to go to the doctor or eat food she plainly doesn't want is likely to make her resentful. As she is unlikely to be a girl who is openly very rebellious and cheeky, her anger could become turned inwards and make her depressed, phobic or obsessional. It could also make her seek more isolation from her close family than is good for her.

But all these are 'worst case scenarios'. At the moment, there is little evidence that would suggest cause for panic. (Even the account of the shopping trip is one most mothers' of teenage girls – and probably many boys too – will recognize!) It will do no harm, and possibly a good deal of good, if Karen's parents tried the following:

- acknowledging that, as a teenage girl, Karen may want to eat different foods from the rest of the family. Allowing her some choice of food at mealtimes, and letting her skip a few, might make staying with the family a more attractive option. Doing this would also give her self-esteem a boost by recognizing her new status as a 'growing young woman', rather than just another one of the 'kids'.

- giving Karen a good leaflet or book on beauty, which includes a section on nutrition and healthy dieting. Girls of this age tend to know everything about the fat and calorie content of foods, but less about their vitamin, mineral and protein content. Remember a gentle 'pull' with objective, convincing information is likely to be more effective than commands such as 'You must eat a meal before you go out.' (See Rule 8.)

- phoning the helpline of a charity dealing with eating disorders to ask for advice on signs to look out for, and keeping their leaflet ready in case she finds that Karen is making herself sick after all. (See Rule 2.)
- making it easier for Karen to find 'space' from her brothers and sisters at home. Screening off her corner of the bedroom and providing her sister with a set of radio headphones might give Karen the peace and privacy she is starting to need. (See Rule 17.)
- sending Karen away on a residential school trip might help to make her less 'clingy' at home and help her to bond more closely with her own peer group. The school can advise on how to find grants if the family's budget is too tight.
- encouraging Karen to look for a weekend or evening part-time job might also build her social skills, as well as helping her to have some time away from home. She has almost reached an age where these will start to become available.
- not contradicting Karen when she declares herself ugly, but giving lots of specific, genuine, positive feedback about her appearance at other times. They could focus their compliments on her hair, eyes and skin, and, of course, her other many good personal qualities and strengths. As an immediate response Pat could just say something which will remind Karen of the damage her self-put-down is doing. For example, *'Calling yourself ugly is a bit unkind, isn't it?'* (See Rule 12.)
- easing up pressure on her to buy clothes. It is highly unlikely that Karen will *want* to stay in her baggy tee-shirts for long, especially if they are not part of the current teen 'uniform'. Treating her to teen fashion magazines from time to time might whet her appetite! (See Rule 18.)
- finding some activity that Eddie and Karen could do on their own together. Perhaps Eddie could take Karen to a science museum or a film, as it seems she doesn't share his interest in football. (See Rule 10.)
- having more fun themselves. Pat in particular sounds as though she could do with some distraction from the family and some 'lightening up'. (See Rule 20.)

'He's C-stream in everything and he knows it':
How can Brian and Jill help?

'By drinking, a boy is … released from the shame and anxiety of seeing himself as little. The adolescent culture of cruelty has it in for any boy who slackens his pace in the race to prove masculinity and drinking puts him up with the "real men".'

Dan Kindlon and Michael Thompson, *Raising Cain – Protecting the Emotional Life of Boys*

Of course both Brian and Jill might be riddled with guilt. And if they are, this could certainly be affecting the way they are handling the situation. They are intelligent, caring people who are likely to have thought long and hard before adopting Sean. Certainly if Sean had any lingering resentment about being adopted, or their marriage problems (which occurred at a crucial age for him), or their 'workaholism', it would be no surprise if it surfaced in this form and in this situation. I have no doubt that Sean could be helped by talking through some of these issues with a counsellor or therapist, or in a self-help group, but I am not so sure that he is ready to do so yet.

Perhaps with hindsight it might have been a mistake to insist on the crammer college at this stage. But I think it would serve little use for Brian and Jill to beat their guilty breasts in Sean's face. He doesn't need to be put into the position of feeling he has to rescue them from a past which they might now regret. If Brian and Jill must face their guilt, they should do so privately, and at a later time. For the moment, they need to put their energies into thinking how they can best help Sean. (When our guilt buttons are pressed, we can knee-jerk into inappropriate action just to make *ourselves* feel better.)

Looking at the positive aspects of this situation, it is a great opportunity for the whole family to do some re-evaluating. In the process of helping Sean to find out what he wants out of life, and how to find it, Brian and Jill might at last discover a better way to live for themselves.

The fact that they are disagreeing about the best way forward for Sean is not a problem. In fact, it could be an advantage. Firstly, debate between two opposing positions often brings forward more creative solutions to problems. Secondly, it is a way of showing Sean that their concern for him can override their need to assert their own individual positions within their marriage. (A perennial problem for this couple – and many others I know!) But, of course, to achieve this kind of settlement of disputes within a family requires TIME!

So what can Brian and Jill actually do to help Sean? They could:

– start by attacking their diaries! Both need to do some heavy rescheduling and delegating in order to free up some time. They are both well established in their careers, so it is unlikely that either would be taking a mammoth risk by saying 'No' to some work commitments. This may not be a crisis in the normal understanding of the word but, as I said earlier, it is a great opportunity for them to re-evaluate their priorities and spend some time together as a family. (See Rule 10.)

– arrange to talk together with Sean. But first, they must listen and listen and listen! Doing this, and setting aside time to be with him, are the most powerful means Brian and Jill have of giving Sean the message that he is valuable in spite of his limitations and aspects of his current behaviour. Reassurances could be received as patronizing in his position, and certainly throwing more money instantly at the problem is unlikely to help. However, they could agree to do some constructive 'spoiling' and decide to do their listening in some enticing place away from home. A weekend away to see an important football match, a last minute skiing or scuba diving holiday together or a trip to a rock festival are the kinds of breaks this family can well afford and teenagers often appreciate! But the main aim of whatever kind of time-out they might take would be to increase their understanding of how Sean is currently 'ticking', and to help Sean himself achieve more insight into what might fire him. They could stimulate him to reflect constructively by asking him questions which would reveal what has made him feel really excited / happy / interested / sad

/ angry / frustrated or bored recently (even if these are just things he has seen on TV or in the pub!) (See Rules 3, 7, 8 and 18.)

– discuss with Sean their dilemma and disagreement about whether or not to give him money to go travelling. (There's no easy 'always right' answer to this one! Much will depend on each family's values about money in general, not to mention their individual financial circumstances.) It would be a good 'life lesson' for Sean to understand and accept that they must find a solution (however imperfect) in spite of this dilemma and disagreement.

– additionally, unless they have done so already, they could consider having a talk with him about alcohol to ensure that he knows its dangers.

– buy him some inspirational, easy-to-read books such as *Making Every Day Count – Daily Readings for Young People on Solving Problems, Setting Goals and Feeling Good About Yourself* by Pamela Espeland and Elizabeth Verdick or *Chicken Soup for the Teenage Soul* by Jack Canfield, Mark Victor Hanson and Kimberly Kirberger.

– research other opportunities for Sean to throw into the decision-making pot. There are now a number of books around containing useful ideas on how to make the best use of a gap year, or they could ask for ideas from friends and their contacts in the charity world. One compromise solution could be a short, interesting work experience that used his people skills, or a supervised voluntary work project overseas. Both would help him discover how much his personality would stand him in good stead in the 'real world'. After this, he could take six months or a year to travel around the world. Brian and Jill could even meet up with him for a few days (as I have known many parents do) in a location which they have always wanted to visit.

– if, on his return, Sean is still unclear about what he wants to do, this might be a better time for an investment in career advice.

But the chances are that the time away will have boosted both Sean's inner and outer confidence. My experience is that this kind of travelling has a very positive effect on young people. I have seen many of them return with their self-esteem, optimism and 'street-wise' assertiveness skills recharged. Sean would certainly meet other young people in his position and would make some close supportive friends. It is also likely that a proportion of his new friends will also have had 'mixed-up' family backgrounds, and the open sharing that this kind of travelling together brings could be very therapeutic.

– while Sean is away, Brian and Jill could work seriously at rebalancing their own lives and finding new dreams for themselves, so that he returns to two happier and well-organized role-models! (See Rules 1 and 20.)

'He's too easily led':
How can Roger and Carol help?

This kind of 'problem' can be very upsetting in a family that has previously had an 'easy ride' through life. Most parents learn how to cope with these kinds of difficulties and anxieties the 'hard way' – that is through experience and trial and error. Roger needs to be reassured that it is more than Okay to ask for help, and that it is also highly sensible to check out problems before they become major crises. Asking for help is obviously something he is not used to doing.

If David has a problem with confidence, it is certainly not very obvious. In fact, some of his behaviour might suggest the opposite. He could just be a lively square peg asserting his identity in a fairly conventional, quiet round hole. But there are indications that he might have a self-esteem problem, so it would be worth checking out. His mixing with much older boys could be his search for more status. Perhaps he is being left out of his peer age group for some reason. If so, this might be opening up an old emotional wound if he has pre-viously felt similar feelings (being a much younger son and being temperamentally different from his brothers and parents, this is possible). Also, skating is not the most common kind of sport for boys to excel in, so maybe there has been some teasing (or even bullying) by friends into more 'macho' pursuits.

Stealing and lying are common behaviours at this age, so it is important that he doesn't become over-hastily labelled by his 'good' family (or anyone else, for that matter) as a 'thief' or a 'liar'. But this behaviour *can* also be a signal that his self-esteem is low. (The 'If I'm bad I might as well act bad' pattern.)

David's rudeness to his mother could be another hint that his sense of his own identity as a budding masculine man needs strengthening. But it is also common at this age for boys to want to pull away from female apron strings. However, his behaviour is aggressive and sug-gests that he is angry. He needs to be helped to find a better outlet for his feelings, even if it turns out that they are justified (for example, he *is* being left out or being bullied).

So, what can Roger and Carol do to help on a practical level? They could:

- join a parenting network group. They would find this supportive in their current difficulties with David. But it would probably also give them a great confidence boost as well. It is likely that they would find that they have been above-average parents and will be able to help others in the group. It is also likely that the group will contain much younger parents as well. They might be gently confronted with the fact that the world that David is mixing in is very different from the one their older boys might have encountered. (See Rule 2.)
- acquire some information on the current drug scene and how to spot tell-tale symptoms of drug use – just in case. If David is as easily led as they think and has already entered the pub scene, they should be on the alert. (It doesn't sound as though this is an angle that is in their mind at the moment.) (See Rule 2.)
- Roger could buy a book or attend a course on anger management. Admitting to his son that he has a problem in this area as well might help. He would then not only be a better role-model, but he would also be able to give David some coaching on how to keep his cool and express himself more assertively. (See Rule 15.)
- talk to the school counsellor or one of David's teachers. They could mention their concerns and ask the school to observe David a little more closely. If there is a sign that bullying might be taking place, teachers need to know. They could also have a word with the person who supervises the skating on Saturdays, or a coach who has helped David in the past. If there has been teasing about the sport, they might be the best people to advise on how to handle it. (See Rule 14.)
- share their concerns with David's older brother, Paul. It may be that he would be happy to take David away for a 'man's weekend'. (I am not qualified to make a more specific suggestion!) These brothers were obviously close in the past.

It could be that David is missing him and would have a big self-esteem boost just from knowing that his older brother set aside some special time for him. (See Rule 10.)

– Carol needs to make it clear to David that she was hurt by his rudeness. Even though he may not admit it openly at the moment, her feelings will undoubtedly matter to him. An appeal to his 'better nature' would be a wise move. We know that they are essentially a close family, and can assume that David basically loves and respects his mother. So this kind of 'pull' approach is likely to be more successful than an embarrassing rap on his knuckles. (See Rule 8.)

– make an action plan of how they would respond if they have more reason to suspect David of lying and stealing. This would have to include confronting him and agreeing to some rules and sanctions. (One of these could be facing him with the possibility that they will inform the school.) Knowing that they had a plan ready should their fears be realized, will reduce their anxiety. (Over-anxious parents are not great confidence-builders!) (See Rule 13.)

'She won't talk about losing her father': How can Isabel help?

'One of the most difficult changes that takes place after a parent dies is the change of roles within the family ... it can take teenagers years to negotiate such changes. But when a parent dies there is no time any more. Suddenly you must act like an adult.'

Rebecca Abrams, *When Parents Die*

It is certainly very common for teenagers whose parents die to lose a great deal of confidence. Tina's immediate practical coping behaviour, her subsequent focus and anxiety around her exams, and her distancing herself from her mother are all common reactions.

As she is still a teenager, we would expect the death of her father to hit her particularly hard for a number of reasons. Firstly, her emotional system was already working under pressure. Her hormones have far from settled down and she also has the stress of competitive exams to manage. Secondly, she was still at an age when she might reasonably expect her home to be a secure safety net should ever she need it. Isabel was, understandably, too overwhelmed by her own grief to be able to comfort or support anyone else. Her brother was an ocean away. Thirdly, Tina had a major life transition forced 'unnaturally' upon her at a time when she was struggling to cope with launching herself into the adult world.

'Mood swings, anger, guilt, depression, impatience and impetuousness are all emotional states common to the bereaved and adolescent. A parent's death is like a double bereavement to a teenager because they are already coping with losing parts of themselves.'

Ellen Noonan, *Counselling Young People*

But in addition to these 'normal' pressures for teenagers who have lost a parent, Tina has further pressures. The fact that her father was a barrister and Tina is planning to read law are special aspects of her situation which need to be considered. She has probably lost the person in the family who she was most like, and who would have been a great support and source of wisdom throughout her career. (And having a lawyer for a daughter, I know how tough even studying for this profession can be, especially when your parents haven't a clue about the issues and dilemmas with which you are faced!)

In short, Tina has lost trust in both herself and the world. She is terrified. It is going to take a long time before her confidence is restored.

For the moment, Isabel shouldn't be worried that Tina's grief is not surfacing. Putting pressure on her to talk about the loss of her father to her or anyone else isn't going to help. In fact, it could dent Tina's confidence even more. She could feel as though she is being selfish, odd or hard-hearted for behaving in the way she is. The truth is that there is no right or wrong way for anyone to handle such a very difficult life experience. There is no comforting blueprint that anyone can offer Isabel and Tina. Essentially, it is a matter of each working their individual way very tentatively through it step-by-step.

This is a very hard position for Isabel to be in. Not only has she lost her husband, she feels she is losing her daughter. As a parent, she is likely to be in a more highly-charged emotional muddle. The naturally ambivalent feelings she would have are going to be even stronger. On the one hand, she wants to see Tina standing firmly on her own two feet as soon as possible, with a law degree to support herself. She wants the extra reassurance that Tina will survive all right. On the other hand, for her own confidence, she herself probably needs to be needed by her daughter.

Perhaps the single most important thing that Isabel can do for her daughter is step back from trying to control her path to recovery. Instead, her main task for now is to continue to strengthen her own confidence and build a new life for herself. Tina more than ever needs her mother to be the 'rock' that she can depend on, especially during the difficult times ahead such as her exams, her move to university, and the inevitable time when her grief will surface.

But having said this, there are many practical ways in which Isabel can support Tina now. She still has a direct active parenting role to play. She can:

- listen attentively to whatever Tina wants to talk about. (See Rule 3.)
- remind Tina (or teach her if she hasn't already done so) how to manage her anxiety over her work and the exams. (See Rule 15.)
- help her to make decisions (rather than giving her advice or making decisions for her). One dilemma that Isabel could help Tina with is whether Tina should take a gap year. Tina is likely to think again about this as an option because the university or her school might well suggest it. At the moment, she is possibly too fragile to make this decision. But later her mother could help her to write a list summarizing the pros and cons similar to the one below. (See Rule 8.)

Should I take a gap year?

Pros

Chance to think again about career – make sure that it is what *I* really want to do

Try placements in other worlds of work

Earn some money

Learn a new language

Meet new friends

Become more independent

Escape the 'sad' family environment without the temptation to run home when the going gets tough (if the year is spent some distance away)

Cons

Get trained more quickly (law is a long haul!)

Going into another learning environment will feel more familiar and less risky than travelling into uncharted territory

Escape the family to go to university, with the safety net of knowing family and friends are not too far away

University has a good, free counselling service

No big, pressurizing decisions to make now about how to spend gap year

> Could take more interesting (and paid) 'year out' after finishing
> degree and before starting training contract or first job

- build Tina's self-esteem by looking at ways she could give her some extra spoiling because she deserves it, and in doing so, they could take some of the extra pressure from her. This could be, for example, extra coaching or a laptop computer so Tina could take her work with her if she wanted to stay with her brother. (See Rule 18.)
- contact the school and find out what kind of support they could offer. Certainly a reasonable expectation would be for the teachers to give her some extra careful monitoring and support. They may also be able to extend deadlines for essays and if her marks fall below those which she should gain, they could write an explanatory paragraph in their references for her university applications and any job that she may apply for.
- help Tina focus and acknowledge (if not celebrate) the smallest of her achievements. (See Rule 19.)
- give Tina some basic information about the process of grief, especially in relation to its physical effects. For example, it might be helpful for her to know that it is quite normal for feelings of grief to sometimes emerge months and months later, and that it usually takes two years for the emotional system in our bodies to stabilize. (I was shocked myself to find just how deeply physical the sensations are. They can be very scary sometimes.)
- make it clear to her that every individual grieves in their own way and her way may be very different from anyone else's in the family.

> 'In response to major loss, both older children and adolescents cry less freely than adults do. A teenager who feels they may "lose it" emotionally sees mourning as a threat.'
>
> Hope Edelman, *Motherless Daughters*

– when Tina is in a state about her homework, resist immediately smothering her anxiety with obvious reassurances. Tina is an intelligent girl who knows what matters and what does not in terms of her school work. Hold back on saying things like: *'You know you'll do it eventually, you always do. And if you don't, don't worry, a late essay is not the most important thing in the world'* or *'You'll pass at the very least. No one expects you to get good grades in these circumstances.'* Instead, just acknowledge how she is feeling and listen and listen. Then suggest that she takes a short break to do something which will calm her anxiety (if only a few stretching and breathing exercises). (See Rules 3 and 15.)

– research extra sources of support before she needs them. Isabel's job as a librarian gives her a great opportunity to do this. For example, she could acquire the kind of information and career advice that Tina's father would have provided. His former colleagues and professional law associations would probably be willing to assist. (See Rule 2.)

– think about buying a copy of Rebecca Abrams' excellent book, *When Parents Die: Learning to Live with the Loss of a Parent*, so that Tina can read it whenever she is ready. People who cannot talk about their loss often gain immense comfort and insight from reading books, such as those written by people who have been through it themselves and also have professional wisdom to share.

In looking after herself and doing her more practical parenting tasks, Isabel will be reinforcing the foundations of Tina's sense of security and her confidence. Her actions will be *indirectly* conveying these three vital reassuring messages:

1. *'I am your mother and I will be here to support you whatever happens. It is OK for you to take the role of a child when you need to. You are a very important and very loveable person however you are behaving or however badly you may do at your exams.'*

2. *'I am strong enough for you to leave home and make your way in the world whenever you are ready for it.'*
3. *'People can survive the pain of deep grief. They can learn to re-experience Joy – even if they will go on missing the person for the rest of their lives. Look – I am the living proof of this.'*

Tina needs to hear and be convinced by all these messages before she starts letting the full range of her confused thoughts and feelings emerge. But in the state she is in, she is more likely to receive them unconsciously when they are conveyed through actions rather than 'head-on' through words.

> 'I stare, dry-eyed and numb, as the coffin slides through the curtains ... in the following days I am haunted by the vision ... I want to run after it, drag it back. I want to lift the lid and demand answers from my father to questions I don't even know how to ask.'
>
> Kate Atkinson, *Behind the Scenes at the Museum*

A Final Word

Well, how did you fare in your angst tests? I have usually found that most parents have much more wisdom than they think they have. I hope this was your experience. If it wasn't, and you still feel in need of more help and guidance, be assured that there is plenty more help readily available.

Firstly, I have compiled a short *Recommended Reading* list which could fill in some of the gaps this short book inevitably has left.

Secondly, you could seek some face-to-face support. In the last ten years or so there has been a rapid increase in this kind of resource for parents of teens. In particular, many parenting associations and adult education centres now offer special courses and workshops. The details of these are almost always given to local libraries, or they are posted on the Internet.

Should you be living in an area which does not offer this kind of help, why not start a self-help support group for parents of teens yourself? You would only need two or three people, a comfortable private room – and a kettle! – to start one. You could use self-help books (such as this one), tapes, videos and material from the Internet to guide your sessions. Most professionals working in the field are more than happy to support this kind of venture. For example, they often give talks, provide meeting venues, help with publicity and suggest reading material.

But a word of warning! Please don't allow any group you are in-volved in to become dreary or depressing. Listening to problem after problem is not what you or anyone else is likely to need. Make sure that at least one person has the task of keeping the focus on solutions and ensuring that you also take time to share your parenting joys and successes. Confidence never flourishes in a negative atmosphere.

For those of you who feel after reading through this book that you are doing a 'good-enough' job at the moment, can I suggest that you hang on to the book for a little while longer – just in case! Unless you are extraordinarily lucky, there are bound to be some moments during these parenting years when you will question whether you are taking the 'right' or 'wrong' approach. (Teenagers are exceptionally adept in both their words and deeds at stirring self-doubt!) The feed-back that I have had from *Confident Children* suggests that it is at these times that books like this are most useful – even if all they do is reassure you that you are on the right track.

I hope that you derive as much pleasure from parenting your teenagers as I did. But in my experience, the greatest rewards come later. There is so much joy and peace of mind to be had in watching our adult children reap the advantages that their confidence un-doubtedly attracts into their lives.

Have fun with your confident teens.

Further Help

Recommended Reading

For Adults

Rebecca Abrams, *When Parents Die: Learning to Live with the Loss of a Parent* (Routledge, 1992)

Kate Atkinson, *Behind the Scenes at the Museum* (Black Swan, 1995)

Robert Bayard and Jean Bayard, *Help! I've got a Teenager* (Exley, 1984)

Helen Bethune, *Positive Parent Power* (Thorsons, 1991)

Judy Blume, *Letters to Judy: What Kids Wish They Could Tell You* (Pan, 1987)

Richard Carlson, *Don't Sweat the Small Stuff with Your Family* (Hodder and Stoughton, 1998)

Steve Chalke, *The Parentalk Guide to the Teenage Years* (Hodder and Stoughton, 1999)

Jean Illsley Clarke, *Self-Esteem: A Family Affair* (Hazelden Information and Educational Services, 1998)

John C. Coleman and Leo B. Hendry, *The Nature of Adolescence* (Routledge, 1999)

Hope Edelman, *Motherless Daughters* (Hodder and Stoughton, 1995)

Jacki Gordon and Gillian Grant, *How We Feel: An Insight into the Emotional World of Teenagers* (Jessica Kingsley, 1997)

Suzanne E. Harrill, *Empowering Teens to Build Self-Esteem* (Innerworks Publishing, 1996)

Dan Kindlon and Michael Thompson, *Raising Cain – Protecting the Emotional Life of Boys* (Penguin Books, 2000)

Gael Lindenfield, *Assert Yourself* (Thorsons, 1986)

___, *Super Confidence* (Thorsons, 1989)

___, *The Positive Woman* (Thorsons, 1992)

___, *Managing Anger* (Thorsons, 1993)

___, *Self Esteem* (Thorsons, 1995)

___, *Self Motivation* (Thorsons, 1996)

___, *Emotional Confidence* (Thorsons, 1997)

___, *Success from Setbacks* (Thorsons, 1999)

___, *Confident Children* (Thorsons, 2000)

___ with Malcolm Vandenburg, *Positive Under Pressure* (Thorsons, 2000)

Aidan Macfarlane and Ann McPherson, *Teenagers: The Agony, The Ecstasy, The Answers* (Little, Brown & Co, 1999)

Sheila Munroe, *Communicating with Your Teenager* (Piccadilly Press, 1998)

Ellen Noonan, *Counselling Young People* (Routledge, 1990)

Lou Ann Smith, *Be Decisive* (Change Your Life Books, 1999)

Laura Sessions Stepp, *Our Last Best Shot: Guiding Our Children Through Early Adolescence* (Riverhead Books, 2000)

Yvette Solomon and John Coleman, *Dealing with Bullying* (Hodder Wayland, 1998)

Laurence Steinberg with Wendy Steinberg, *Crossing Paths: How Your Child's Adolescence Triggers Your Own Crises* (Simon and Schuster, 1994)

Ved Varma, *Troubles of Children and Adolescents* (Jessica Kingsley, 1997)

For Teenagers

Jack Canfield, Mark Victor Hansen and Kimberly Kirberger, *Chicken Soup for the Teenage Soul* (Vermillion, 1999)

Sean Covey, *The Seven Habits of Highly Effective Teens* (Simon and Schuster, 1998)

Pamela Espeland and Elizabeth Verdick, *Making Every Day Count: Daily Readings for Young People on Solving Problems, Setting Goals, and Feeling Good About Yourself* (Free Spirit Publishing, 1998)

Anne Frank, *Diary of a Young Girl* (Puffin Books, 1997)

Jay McGraw, *Strategies for Teens* (Fireside, 2000)

Cassandra Walker Simmons, *Becoming Myself* (Free Spirit Publishing, 1994)

Sue Townsend, *The Secret Diary of Adrian Mole Aged 13^3/$_4$* (Mandarin, 1989)

Useful Internet Sites

National Parenting and Family Institute
www.e-parents.org
This site will give you advice on which parenting organization would be most helpful.

Trust for the Study of Adolescence
www.tsa.uk.com
Trust for the Study of Adolescence publishes and sells books and runs courses.

Words of Discovery
www.wordsofdiscovery.com
This site specializes in books to nurture children's personal growth.

Cassettes

Gael Lindenfield has made a number of personal-development cassettes which could be helpful for parents of teenagers. Each is designed as a self-help programme of exercises to be used on a regular basis. The list of titles includes:

- *Self Motivation* (Thorsons, 1997)
- *Self Esteem* (Thorsons, 1998)
- *Success from Setbacks* (Thorsons, 1999)
- *Managing Emotions at Work* (Thorsons, 1999)
- *Emotional Confidence* (Thorsons, 2000)

These cassettes are available at all good bookshops, or direct from Thorsons (telephone 0870 900 2050 or 0141 306 3349).

About the author

You can contact Gael Lindenfield through her publishers at the following address:

Gael Lindenfield c/o Thorsons
HarperCollins*Publishers*
77–85 Fulham Palace Road
Hammersmith
London W6 8JB
United Kingdom

Or you can contact her directly by email:
lindenfield.office@btinternet.com
For further information about Gael Lindenfield, go to her website:
www.gael-lindenfield.com

Index